W9-DAM-370

the SUPER simple guide to LANDSCAPING
Your Garden Pond

Muha, Kurtz, Paletta

t.f.h.

T.F.H. Publications, Inc.

© 2004 T.F.H. Publications, Inc.

Distributed in the UNITED STATES to the Pet Trade by T.F.H. Publications, Inc., 1 TFH Plaza, Neptune City, NJ 07753; on the Internet at www.tfh.com; in CANADA by Rolf C. Hagen Inc., 3225 Sartelon St., Montreal, Quebec H4R 1E8; Pet Trade by H & L Pet Supplies Inc., 27 Kingston Crescent, Kitchener, Ontario N2B 2T6; in ENGLAND by T.F.H. Publications, PO Box 74, Havant PO9 5TT; in AUSTRALIA AND THE SOUTH PACIFIC by T.F.H. (Australia), Pty. Ltd., Box 149, Brookvale 2100 N.S.W., Australia; in NEW ZEALAND by Brooklands Aquarium Ltd., 5 McGiven Drive, New Plymouth, RD1 New Zealand; in SOUTH AFRICA by Rolf C. Hagen S.A. (PTY.) LTD., P.O. Box 201199, Durban North 4016, South Africa; in Japan by T.F.H. Publications. Published by T.F.H. Publications, Inc.

Library of Congress Cataloging-in-Publication Data
Muha, Laura.
The super simple guide to landscaping your garden pond / Laura Muha, Jeffrey Kurtz, and Michael Paletta.
p. cm.
Includes index.
ISBN 0-7938-3452-X (alk. paper)
1. Water gardens. I. Kurtz, Jeffrey. II. Paletta, Michael S. III.
Title.
SB423.M824 2004
635.9'674--dc22
2003024942

Contents

Part One: Landscaping Considerations 7

Chapter 1: The Practicalities. 9

Location 10

Filtration 14

Lighting 19

Minimum depth 22

Chapter 2: Setting the Scene 27

Formal pond designs 28

Informal ponds 30

Wildlife pond designs 33

Fishpond designs 36

Before You Dig!

Chapter 3: Waterfalls, Cascades and Streams 37

Setting up and running a waterfall properly 38

Ready, Set, Dig! 40

Pumps for Waterfalls 42

Using streams 45

Part Two: Styles & Types 51

Chapter 4: Formal Garden Pond Design 53

The Formal Pond on an Informal Budget 55

Examples of fine formal water gardens 57

Statuary in the Formal Water Garden 60

The Freestanding Fountain 62

Other Ornaments and Accents
for Formal Water Gardens 64

Chapter 5: Informal Water Garden Design 67

It's the Natural Thing to do 68

The Finer Points of Informal Ponds 69

Practical Solutions to Creating
Informal Water Gardens 70

Making Connections: The Informal
Garden Stream 75

Accents and Ornaments for
the Informal Water Garden 77

Chapter 6: Color in the Water Garden. 81

The Many Moods of Color 82

Chapter 7: The Oriental Water Garden

Chinese and Japanese Influences 90

Ornaments and Accents for the

Oriental Water Garden 92

The Koi Pond 94

Part Three: Your Pond in Nature **103**

Chapter 8: A Pond for All Seasons 105

Trees 106

Bushes and Shrubs 108

Perennials and Annuals .109

Rooted Emergent Plants 111

Floating Emergent Plants 116

Marginals 120

Planting Suggestions 126

Chapter 9: A Walk on the Wild Side 129

Attracting Wildlife to Your Pond 130

Chapter 10: Designer ponds—Making a Pond Unique 145

Creating Your Own Style 146

Optional Water Features 149

Know
Your
Plants

Resources 155

Index 157

Photo Credits 160

Part One
Landscaping Considerations
by Laura Muha

"You know, Maybe garden ponds just aren't our thing."

The Practicalities

Now that you've decided to put in a pond, you're undoubtedly itching to get started. Well, drop that shovel! Doing a little homework before you start digging can make the difference between a water garden that's a success and one that's a disappointment–or worse, an expensive headache.

It takes time and patience to cultivate water gardens like this one.

The first thing you should do is to ask yourself a few questions about your goals. Do you plan to keep plants, fish, or both? Do you envision a pond that looks as if it was tucked into your yard by Mother Nature herself, or one that would be more at home in the garden of a stately English manor house? If you don't already have a clear picture of what you want, skip ahead to the next chapter for a description of the various types of ponds and what's involved in building and maintaining them. Clip pictures from magazines, browse the display ponds at your local aquatic store, and ask friends and neighbors if you can check out their water features.

Location

Once you have an idea of what kind of pond you want, it's time to figure out where to put it. There are very few places where it's impossible to put a pond—you can even create one in your living room using a pre-formed plastic shell—but there are definitely some places that work better than others. Here are a few things to take into consideration when evaluating potential locations for your pond.

Formal water gardens fit well on patios or decks where they can be viewed from several angles.

View

The whole point of building a pond is to enjoy it, right? So make sure to locate yours in a place where you can do that easily—and not just when you're outdoors. Wouldn't it be nice to be able to gaze out at the water from your home office or meditate on it though the kitchen window while cooking dinner? (That's especially important if you live in colder climates, where a window view may be the closest you get to your pond for up to half the year.)

Here's a hint

Use rope or your garden hose to outline the approximate size and shape of a pond in the location you have in mind. Leave it there for a day or two, and look at it from all angles. Can you see it easily from the places where you spend the most time?

When evaluating locations, also consider how close they are to electrical outlets and hose spigots. If you dream of a fish pond in a secluded glen, are you willing to go to the expense of running an electrical cable under an acre of lawn to power your filter and pump? Or to drag your hose the same distance every time you need to top off your pond (which is likely to be more often than you think)?

Terrain

In nature, ponds tend to be found at low spots in the landscape, where water accumulates naturally. But installing a pond at the lowest point in your yard isn't a good idea, because every time it rains, water will wash down the slope into your pond, carrying with it pesticides and fertilizers that can sicken fish and cause algae blooms. Plus, water that soaks into the ground around your pond can build up under your liner, causing it to bubble or erode the soil that supports it, collapsing your pond. That's not to say you can't put a pond at the base of a slope, but you do have to be prepared to work with it by elevating the edge of your pond so it doesn't get flooded or by finding a way to divert the runoff.

Sunlight

If you want to grow aquatic plants, such as water lilies, your pond will need five to six hours of direct sunlight a day in order for them to thrive. However, if it gets much more than that, the pond may become overgrown with algae and the water may get so warm that it stresses fish. Of course, many ponds—especially very large ones—don't get straight sunlight for part of the day followed by straight shade for the rest; rather, they get a combination of both all day long. If that's the case in your yard, then try for a 6:4 ratio of shade to sun—that is, aim for a location where about 60 percent of your pond will be shaded and 40 percent will be in direct sun for most of the day.

Ponds exposed to full sunlight are good candidates for lush plant growth.

How can you figure that out? Well, remember that hose trick we told you about a minute ago? You can also use it to assess how much sun a pond will get. Outline the shape of a pond on the site where you're thinking about putting one, but this time watch how the light moves across it at different times of day. You can even put stakes in the ground at the edge of the shadow

Part 1

and write the time on them. If you do this a number of times during the course of the day, it won't take long to figure out whether your site meets your needs light-wise.

Trees

We've suggested you locate your pond in a location where it will get at least some shade, but don't try to set it at the foot of a tree. Picturesque as it might look, the roots will make digging difficult now and could rip or crack your liner later. Worse, trees shed all sorts of things–petals and seeds in the spring, leaves in the fall–and all of them are going to land in your pond, turning it into a mainte-nance nightmare. Decomposing leaves will create a slimy mess that pollutes your water and clogs your filter. Plus, the foliage of some trees, including weeping willows and black walnuts, can be toxic to fish. So while shade is good, trees too close to a pond are often not.

Leaves blown into a pond can alter its water chemistry.

Permits and Regulations

Before starting to dig, check with your municipality because some towns have ordinances that apply to ponds. They may have to be located a certain distance from your property line, for instance, or you may be required to file for a permit before starting to dig. Some towns require fences around ponds over a certain depth. Make sure you know your municipality's regulations before starting your project, because you don't want to go to all the trouble and expense of installing a pond, only to be informed that you have to move it. And while you're at it, call your utility companies to make sure there are no gas, phone, electrical, or water lines running through your proposed pond site.

Filtration

Now that you've selected a location for your pond, it's time to talk equipment–specifically filters. Some people argue that it's not necessary to filter ponds–after all, Mother Nature doesn't. But Mother Nature also doesn't line her ponds with rubber, stock them with as many fish as most of us put in our garden ponds, or feed them as heavily, causing them to produce excessive waste that pollutes the water.

In other words, if you're planning to keep fish, you should definitely filter your pond. If you're not, it's still worth considering, because filters can also help keep the water in plant-only ponds clear.

The purpose of a filter is to remove undesirable things–both visible and invisible–from your pond water, keeping it clean and healthy for your fish. If your pond is small enough and you have only one or two fish, you could accomplish the same thing by replacing a large portion of the water every day. But because people are willing to go to that kind of trouble–or able to, in large ponds–the only alternative if you want your fish to be happy and healthy is to use a filter.

There are two types of filtration you'll need in your pond: mechanical filtration and biological filtration.

Mechanical Filtration

Mechanical filtration is the removal of solids, such as fish wastes and dirt particles, from your water. Most filters accomplish this in one of two ways: by trapping the particles in some sort of filtering material, such as foam, or letting them settle out with the help of gravity, so they can be removed later.

Biological Filtration

Biological filtration is harder to explain because it's not something you can see, but it's even more cru-cial than mechanical filtration to the health of your fish. Basically, biological filters consist of bacteri-al colonies that break down waste products, such as ammonia, that are produced by fish. Without these bacteria, the waste would build up in the water, poisoning your fish. You can't buy these bacterial colonies (although

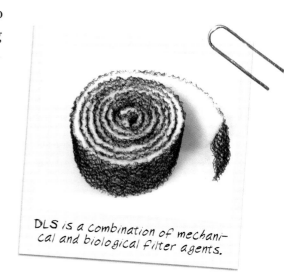

DLS is a combination of mechani-cal and biological filter agents.

there are products on the market that encourage them to grow), but they'll develop naturally in your pond if you give them with a place to live. Some commercial filters provide this in the form of compartments that can be filled with biomedia–materials such as special, plastic beads that provide plenty of surface area for the bacteria to grow on. Others incorporate materials such as sponges that not only provide plenty of places for bacteria to set up housekeeping but also simultaneously provide mechanical filtration.

If you've ever had a fish tank, you probably know that there is a third type of filtration called chemical filtration, which uses substances such as carbon to absorb or neutralize water contaminants. This type of filtration is rarely used in ponds, however, because the other two filters take care of most of the load.

While it's possible to build your own filter, most beginning pond keepers find it easier to buy one. There are too many designs available to discuss in detail here; your local aquatics store can help you determine which model best meets your needs. But whatever filter you choose, make sure that it provides both biological and mechanical filtration and that it's big enough to turn over the water in your pond at least once an hour. This will be indicated as "gallons per hour" or "GPH" on the packaging. And by the way, there's nothing wrong with buying a filter made for a pond a little larger than the one you plan to build–there's no such thing as too much filtration.

Although some filters can be placed directly in the water, most

Part 1

pond keepers prefer external ones because they're easier to clean and provide more of the oxygen needed for the biological filter. If you choose an external filter, you'll have to dig a sump for it to sit in; if the water level inside your filter isn't even with the level in your pond, the filter will overflow. When positioning your filter, don't forget appearance: You can tuck it behind plants or rocks or hide it inside a waterfall.

Pumps

You're going to need a way to get water from your pond into your filter. That's where pumps come in. There are two basic types: those that sit in the bottom of your pond and push water up to your filter, and those that that sit outside the pond and pull the water into it. External pumps are more powerful, but submersible pumps are quieter, less expensive, and will work fine for all but the largest of ponds. The one drawback is that because they sit in the pond, they suck in muck along with water. For that reason, they're often fitted with pre-filters—a piece of foam or other screening material that prevents pieces of pond plants, seeds, and other large chunks of debris from getting sucked into the pump and damaging it. The problem is that the pre-filter material tends to

Large pumps will be needed to push water uphill or over a tall waterfall.

clog, so expect to have to clean it regularly. Alternatively, you can buy a pump built to chop up solids; they don't need pre-filters, but they cost more.

Make sure you purchase a pump that's the right size for your filter. It won't do you any good if your filter can handle 500 gallons an hour, but your pump can only deliver half that much water. Pumps, like filters, usually have a GPH rating marked on the package.

Ultraviolet Sterilizers

These ultraviolet lights are either built into your filter or housed in a separate unit that can be attached to it. As water passes beneath the light, it kills suspended algae cells, helping to eliminate the problem of murky, green water. Many manufacturers claim that these devices are all that are needed to keep your water crystal clear, and they definitely do help. However, even the best UV filter in the world won't keep up with the algae blooms that occur as the result of too much sunlight or overfeeding of fish. In addition, ultraviolet bulbs lose their effectiveness over time, so plan on replacing them at least once a season.

Skimmers

A skimmer is a special filter that uses a pump to draw water from the surface of your pond into a chamber where leaves and other floating debris become trapped. This makes them easy to remove before they decompose in your pond, pollute the water, or get sucked into the filter, clogging it. You don't have to have a skimmer, but many pond keepers find them very useful, especially in areas with a lot of trees.

Lighting

Interior designers know that the right lighting can add atmosphere to even the most ordinary room, casting dramatic shadows on walls, making ceilings look higher, and making attractive architectural features pop out. Good room lighting can set a mood that's cheerful, romantic, or relaxing.

The same is true of pond lights. You can use lighting in or around your pond to turn a fountain into a spray of sparkling diamonds, highlight a statue, or simply to give an ethereal glow to the water. Of course, you don't *have* to light your pond at all, but wouldn't it be nice to be able to enjoy it long after the sun has gone down? And don't forget that lighting the area around your pond will make it easier to navigate safely in the dark.

When designing your lighting plan, keep in mind that the point isn't to make your pond look as if it were in broad daylight hours after the sun has set. Too many lights will wash out shadows that would otherwise add interest. Instead, pick out a special feature or two–a waterfall, perhaps, or a statue–and use lights to set them off. You might want to backlight plants so they cast dramatic shadows on a garden wall, or add low accent lights along the path leading up to your pond.

If you've ever visited a lighting store while redecorating your home, you know that there is a bewildering array of choices available–something that's also true of pond lighting. You can buy lights that sit directly on the floor of your pond, lights that can be mounted on the side of your pond, lights that can be attached to your pump, and lights that can be hung from trees–not to mention rock-shaped lights, floating lights shaped like water lilies, and lights attached to machines that create clouds of fog on the surface of your pond. Your pond shop will be able advise you on what lights to use to achieve different effects, but here are a few things to think about to get you started.

There are two basic ways to illuminate your pond: from below the surface of the water and from above it. (Many people choose a combination of both.)

Submersible Lights

Submersible lights are specially sealed units that rest on the floor of your pond or mount on its side. They can be placed under a water-fall, turning it into a ribbon of light, or in the basin of a fountain, creating a glittering spray; submerged beams of light directed across the pond will give the water a magical glow. Some submersible lights have to be completely under water in order to prevent them from overheating, while others can be used both above and below the surface; make sure you know which one you're buying. One of the biggest drawbacks to submersible lights is that algae can build up on their lenses and dull their lights, so you may need to clean them regularly; take this into account if you're the type who hates maintenance. Plus, submersible lights tend to look prettiest in clear water; if yours is murky, the underwater beams of light will be, too. One last note on submersible lights: If you have fish, try to leave a few dark areas where they can hide– after all, you wouldn't like it if a spotlight were shining into your bedroom all night.

Submersible lights can be used to effectively light up certain features at night.

Surface Lighting

Surface lighting is more adjustable than underwater lighting. It can take many forms, but spotlights are probably the most common. These are single beams of light that can be directed at a specific pond feature–a statue, say, or a waterfall–to set it off, or they can be grouped together to illuminate a larger area. You can also direct them at plants to create dramatic shadows against a wall or building or at a canopy of leaves above your pond to gently illuminate the area below. Spotlights are most commonly white, but you can top them with colored lenses if you want to change the look. Take care when placing spotlights, so they won't shine directly in the eyes of viewers. And look for lights with dark casings, which will be less visible during the daylight.

Safety First

Regardless of the form of lighting that you choose, there are a few technical and safety issues you will have to take into account. Because most pond lights are low voltage–usually 12V to 24V–you will probably have to buy one or more transformers to reduce the voltage of the electricity coming from your electrical main. Make sure you check the voltage on your pond lights, and buy a transformer that matches it. Some transformers can handle only one light, while others can handle several; check the package to be sure.

Also remember that water and electricity are a dangerous combination, so make sure all lighting you use around your pond is specifically for outdoor or pond use, and make sure that any lights you plan to use in the pond are specifically labeled submersible. Also, check with your municipality to find out whether you need an electrical permit to install them. Electrical codes require that outdoor lighting have ground fault circuit interrupters, or GFCIs, to trip the power if a fault is detected.

Minimum Depth

The depth of your pond should depend on two things: what you plan to keep in it and the climate you live in. If you're building a reflecting pool, for instance, or planning a pond that will contain nothing more than a few floating plants, such as water hyacinth, 6 to 12 inches of water will be fine. But if you're planning to keep fish and/or plants such as water lilies, you must take into account their needs when deciding on the depth of your pond.

Aquatic Plants Only

Aquatic plants are a bit like a group of people hanging out at a swimming pool: Some like the deep end, others prefer to stick only their toes in the water, and still others enjoy being near the water, but never climb into it.

When designing a plants-only pond, you'll need to have some idea of which types of plants you want to include (see the last section of this book for suggestions) and plan its depth accordingly. Lilies, for instance, grow best when their crown–the part of the plant where the stem meets the rhizome–is 12 to 18 inches below the surface of the water. The yellow, rod-shaped flower known as Golden Club, or *Orontium aquaticum,* on the other hand, prefers water that's between 3 and 12 inches deep.

Don't allow your pond to become a mass of floating plants; it's not healthy for the pond.

If you're using a pre-formed pond shell, select one with shelves at varying levels to accommodate plants with different needs–perhaps one that's 18 inches deep in the middle for your lilies, with shelves at 6 and 12 inches for other plants.

If you're using a flexible liner, you can excavate your pond in such a way as to include similar shelves, or go deeper in one portion of the pond for lilies and gently slope the other banks to accommodate plants that prefer shallower waters. Keep in mind that many plants, including lilies, prefer calmer water; so keep the deepest area of the pond, where they'll be located, away from waterfalls or fountains.

Fish Ponds

Goldfish, shubunkin, and koi can handle a wide temperature range, as long as it doesn't swing too quickly between extremes. If your pond is too shallow, the water will heat up quickly on a summer day and then plummet along with the air temperature at night, stressing your fish. In the winter, shallow ponds can freeze solid. Needless to say, that wouldn't be very good for your fish!

Koi ponds are usually barren of floating plants, as koi like to snack on their roots.

If you're planning on keeping goldfish, aim for a minimum depth of 2 feet, and if you want to keep koi, aim for 4 feet; if you can go a little deeper that's even better. That will keep the temperature relatively stable during the summer and should be deep enough to eliminate the risk of freezing completely in all but the most extreme of northern climates. Deeper water also gives fish a place to escape predators such as raccoons and herons, which often make regular appearances at garden ponds.

That's not to say your koi pond or goldfish pond has to be the same depth everywhere. If you excavate a pond with terraced sides, you could include, say one 4-foot section where fish can escape the heat of the day in summer and hibernate in winter. The sides could be shallower – perhaps only 18 inches or so.

If you plan to bring your fish inside during the cold months, you can go a little bit shallower – but still aim for a minimum of 18 inches for goldfish and 3 feet for koi.

Setting the Scene

Ponds aren't a one-size-fits-all proposition. Just as some people prefer to furnish their homes with Louis XIV antiques while others like Danish modern, some pond keepers gravitate toward natural-looking water features, while others prefer a highly sculpted or formal look.

What follows are general

Flexible liners give you much more freedom when designing a pond.

descriptions of the basic types of ponds. However, they're just guidelines–if none of them sounds quite right for you or your home, there's no reason you have to stick rigidly within one of the categories. Just incorporate elements of any or all of them to come up with a style all your own. The only thing that really matters is that you're happy.

Formal Pond Designs

A formal pond is usually designed to be the centerpiece of a patio, garden, or section of garden. Geometrically shaped, it is typically surrounded by a precisely fitted border of brick, stone, or tile, and often contains a fountain or statue. But within those parameters, there's a lot of room for interpretation. Think of a lily pond in the garden of an English manor house, a tiled fountain in the courtyard of a Moorish palace, a carved marble fish spouting water into a marble basin on the veranda of an Italianate mansion, the reflecting pool on the mall in Washington, D.C. They're very different from each other, but they're all examples of formal water gardens.

Depicted here is a classic formal style water garden complete with planted containers.

Unlike informal ponds, which are meant to look natural, formal ponds don't make any attempt to hide the fact that they're man-made. A formal pond can have raised edges, be set at ground level, or even below it for a sunken effect. Whatever the setting, the formal pond has a tidy, "everything in its place" feel to it. The two words that describe just about every aspect of this type of water garden are symmetry and precision.

Shape and Size

Formal garden pools can be round, square, octagonal, rectangular, or semicircular. They can be shaped like four-leafed clovers, semi-circles, keyholes, or Moorish stars–to name just a few of the common designs. Because the shapes are always geometric, some people claim that planning a formal pool is easier than coming up with a design for an informal pond, where fewer rules apply. But the symmetry that makes formal ponds arguably simpler to design makes them much more complicated to execute, because there is no room for error. Round ponds have to be perfectly round; clover-shaped ponds have to have lobes that are exactly equal, and the edges of square and rectangular ponds have to be perfectly parallel–not only to each other, but to the edges of any nearby buildings. If they're not, you'll notice every time you look at your pond, and the precise, controlled effect that you're after will be ruined.

When it comes to the size of a formal pond, it's usually better to go bigger than smaller, because the reflective properties of the water play an important part in the overall effect–and the larger the pond, the more mirror-like water surface there will be. Just make sure the pond is proportionate to the area you're going to put it in. If it's too small, it will get lost; if it's too large, it will take over the space the way a king-sized bed takes over a tiny room.

Informal ponds can be incorporated into almost any landscape.

Informal Ponds

Unlike a formal pond, which typically stands alone at the center of a lawn or garden, an informal pond is designed to blend into the landscape as if Mother Nature placed it there herself. Informal ponds usually have curved edges and an irregular shape and are surrounded by a lush growth of plants, just as they would be in nature.

This is probably the most popular type of pond right now, because its relaxed feel goes well with today's relaxed lifestyle. The paradox of such a pond, however, is that achieving its natural, unplanned look requires a lot of planning. Here are some things to think about when designing an informal pondscape.

Shape and Size

A pond in nature doesn't have straight edges or a perfectly symmetrical shape, and neither should an informal pond in your garden. Rather, aim for graceful contours and slightly irregular borders.

If you're using a flexible liner, you can custom-design your pond by laying a length of rope or your garden hose on the ground, connecting the ends, and then adjusting the outline until you come up with a shape that you think will work. Leave it for a day or two and look at it from various angles and locations to make sure you like it; if not, move the hose around again until you get something that works better.

If you prefer to use a pre-formed shell for your pond, you shouldn't have any trouble finding one that's appropriate for an informal design. A kidney- or dumbbell-shaped shell works well for this type of pond, but your local aquatics center will stock many other shapes that will also work. Just steer clear of shells that are perfectly round, square, or rectangular–they won't look natural in an informal scheme.

If you don't have room for a bog or rock garden or don't like the idea, you can use plants to soften the margins of your pond and make it look more natural.

Plants

A pond in nature is almost always surrounded by lush and varied vegetation. The same is true of informal garden ponds. In fact, it's safe to say that plants are probably the single most important element in this type of design, connecting the pond to the surrounding landscape.

Unlike a formal pond, in which plants are arranged symmetrically, plants in an informal pond shouldn't look like they've been

Part 1

The red flowers of Lobelia cardinalis contributed to its popularity as a marginal plant species.

arranged at all. But that doesn't mean you should just throw them anywhere. The best informal ponds have a sort of unstudied elegance to them that is actually a product of forethought and planning.

There are three types of plants that you're likely to use in an informal pond: those that grow in the water, those that grow at its margins, and those that grow on the banks. There are too many of each to talk about them in detail here. However, we can talk about general design principles.

First, think of your pond as a piece of three-dimensional artwork, and select plants that will relate to each dimension: foreground, middle, and rear of your pond. Height is one important consideration in doing this: Shorter plants should go closer to the edge of the pond, perhaps even trailing gracefully into the water. Taller plants should go toward the rear, and mid-height plants can be situated between the two. When buying plants, make sure you know how big they'll be at maturity; that cute little puff of ornamental grass that was perfect at pond's edge at the beginning of the summer can turn into a 6-foot-tall, view-obscuring monster by season's end.

You should also think about color – not just of the blooms, but also of the leaves themselves. If you include too many variegated-leaf plants and the banks of your pond will look like a crazy quilt. Limit yourself to one or two variegated plants, which will provide contrast to the other vegetation.

After you bring your plants home, place them, still in their pots, on the ground around the pond and move the pots around until you get an arrangement that you like. If you were putting together a formal pond, you might arrange your plants to form concentric rings of colors. In an informal design, you shouldn't want to do anything that deliberate–but you can cluster them for impact. A grouping of a half-dozen purple irises will have much more impact, for instance, than those same six plants spread around the edges of your pond.

Finally, think about the lifecycle of each plant. Some bloom early in the season, while others flower later. Gardeners know that the key to a beautiful garden is to include plants that peak at different times, so when one is beginning its decline, another is getting ready to take its place. That way, there's always something interesting to look at.

Wildlife Ponds

If you envision dragonflies flitting across the surface of your pond and deer gathering at water's edge for drink at dusk, a wildlife pond

Apples added to your wildlife pond will surely attract various species of mammals.

could be for you. This is really a variation of an informal pond; so many of the things discussed in the previous section on informal ponds apply here. But because the purpose of the pond is to provide a habitat–or rather, a series of interwoven habitats–for birds, mammals, amphibians, and insects, there are some additional things that must be taken into account.

Edges and Borders

While pre-fabricated shells work very well for informal ponds, if your goal is to attract wildlife, it's better to use a flexible liner. The reason: Pre-formed ponds tend to have steep, slippery sides, which make it hard for wildlife to get into–or out of–the water. Many people who've used pre-formed shells have had the experience of going outside in the morning and finding a mouse or chipmunk that tumbled into the water while trying to get a drink has drowned because it couldn't climb out again. If you use a liner, you can control the grade of the pond basin.

It's also important to heavily plant the side and back edges of a wildlife pond. (You can leave the front open for viewing.) Not only does this look more natural, but it also helps to protect birds and small mammals from predators, such as raccoons, herons, and cats.

Fish in Wildlife Ponds

While some people include fish in their wildlife ponds, it's generally not recommended–at least if you're serious about attracting dragonflies, frogs, and other aquatic life–because fish will eat them. (And by the way, some frogs have also been known to eat fish and even small mammals.) In addition, keeping fish requires a filter and pump,

The pumpkinseed sunfish, Lepomis gibbosus, is a popular but aggressive species of native fish.

which can suck in tadpoles. If you have your heart set on fish, set up your pond specifically for that purpose.

Stocking Your Wildlife Pond

One of the nice things about a wildlife pond is that you don't have to stock it. All you have to do is build it and wait. Birds, frogs, turtles, dragonflies, butterflies, chipmunks, and other wildlife will soon figure out that it's there. Be patient. While you'll start to see some wildlife appearing soon after you install your pond, you can't rush the process; it may take a couple of years before the pond habitat matures enough to attract and support a full complement of wildlife.

One thing you can do to kick-start the process is to add a bucket of mud and water from an established pond; it will contain thousands of the microorganisms that your pond needs to be healthy. Just make sure the water doesn't contain fish eggs, or you could find yourself searching for homes for unwanted fry.

Fish Ponds

Appearance isn't everything when it comes to fishponds. In fact, it's decidedly secondary. That's not to say that you can't have a beautiful fishpond–you can. But your first priority when designing it should be to create the conditions necessary to keep your fish healthy and happy. For the most part, that means keeping their environment clean and stable by filtering the water, making sure to not overstock your pond, filtering the water, making sure the water temperature doesn't go too high or too low, providing shady spots for your fish to hide in, and protecting them from predators.

Waterfalls, Cascades, and Streams

A waterfall or stream in a water garden does more than just fill the air with relaxing burbling sounds. It also aerates and helps to filter the pond. Plus, channeling the outflow from your main filter through the streambed or waterfall provides a natural-looking way to return it to your pond.

Streams that feature large rocks or boulders will help aerate the water.

A successful waterfall or stream requires some planning, preferably while you're designing the pond itself. You don't have to build everything at the same time–it's fine to construct a pond in stages over a period of years–but it's easier (and ultimately less expensive) to do the electric and plumbing lines for future additions during the initial pond construction.

Setting Up and Running a Waterfall Properly

First, the easiest way to set up a waterfall is to buy a kit, complete with a pre-formed spillway and pump, and simply set it up at the edge of your pond. Then position rocks and plants around it make it look as realistic as possible.

The problem is that it's hard to make pre-formed waterfalls–at least the larger ones–look like a natural part of the landscape. Instead, many pond keepers opt to build their own waterfalls from liner and rocks. It requires some planning, but it's not that hard.

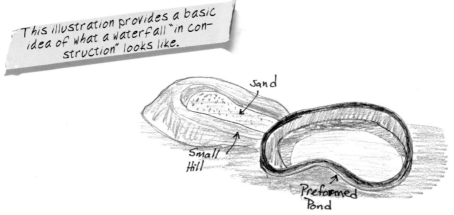

This illustration provides a basic idea of what a waterfall "in construction" looks like.

Sand

Small Hill

Preformed Pond

The first thing to do is to take a good look at your pond site. You can't have a waterfall without something for the water to fall from, so you'll need some sort of slope; how large and steep it is will depend at least partly on the type of waterfall you want. Do you envision lacy ribbons of water flowing through a series of terraced pools—a design that will require a longer, more gradual slope? (Technically speaking, this sort of waterfall is called a cascade, although for purposes of this discussion, we'll use the terms "waterfall" and "cascade" interchangeably.) Or perhaps you picture a more dramatic drop, which will require a steeper hill. Keep in mind that a garden pond is not the place to try and create Niagara Falls in miniature; even if it looked natural (which it won't) the force of the water crashing into your pond would make it too turbulent for plants and fish.

If your site doesn't include a natural slope, you can use dirt from your pond excavation to build up the grade. Just be sure it melds

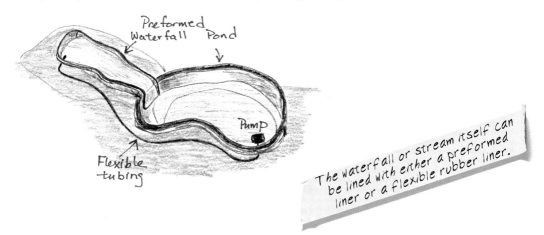

Preformed
Waterfall   Pond

Pump

Flexible
tubing

The waterfall or stream itself can be lined with either a preformed liner or a flexible rubber liner.

smoothly into the contours of the landscape surrounding it–a gentle slope will look more natural than a large mound poking up behind your pond.

If you're creating the slope yourself, it's crucial to either tamp the dirt down completely or let it settle for three months. Otherwise, you could go to all the trouble of getting your waterfall up and running only have it damaged when the ground sinks beneath it.

Ready, Set, Dig!

Before excavating the watercourse, outline its parameters by marking them with stakes every foot or so and connecting the stakes with string. Then, dig between the stakes to create the channel for the waterfall. The sides of the channel can be roughly parallel, or you can make the watercourse wider at the bottom than it is at the top, creating the illusion that the waterfall is larger than it really is. (During the landscaping stage of the project, you can reinforce this impression by using larger stones at the bottom than at the top.)

If you want terraces or pools, cut the steps into the watercourse. The "tread" of each step should lean backward slightly, away from your pond, so water cascading down from the terrace above it will pool there before spilling over to the next level.

At the top of your waterfall, be sure to leave room for a header pool. This is a small basin where water from the pump collects before overflowing into the waterway. You can dig a small sump and fit it with a liner, or just make a header pool out of a plastic bucket, basin, or a small pre-formed pond shell set into the ground. Whatever container you select, make sure it's at least 10 inches deep.

You could, of course, just direct your pump's outflow hose into the waterway, but using a header pool will create a more natural-looking flow because the water will fan out along the lip of the basin before it courses downhill.

Some people also place a similar basin containing gravel or pebbles at the foot of the waterfall. Not only does it create a nicer-looking flow, it will also serve as a collection basin for any debris that washes down your waterfall, making it easy to remove.

Once you've dug out the waterway, coat it with a layer of carpet, newspaper, or sand to prevent rocks from puncturing your liner. Then, fit the liner on top of it. If you have to piece sections of the liner together, start at the pond end of the waterfall and work backward, with uppers section of liner overlapping the lower ones. Then glue them to each other using silicone adhesive. Make sure the liner extends over each side of the waterfall by at least a foot; if not, water may splash out of the waterway and get under the liner. You can hide the edges of the liner with rock.

One of the most fun decisions you'll make about your waterfall is which type of weir or spill stone to use. The weir is the actual lip that the water flows over as it drops into your pond, and its size and shape will determine what appearance of the water as it falls. A single, smooth stone, for instance, creates a satiny curtain of water. (Make sure that this type of weir is level, or you'll get a spout-like effect.) A cluster of rocks will create a frothier, rougher waterfall. If you have numerous terraces in your waterfall, you may want to include a weir at each level.

Pumps for Waterfalls

In nature, rivers or natural springs supply waterfalls with their water. In water gardens, they're supplied by pumps that pull water from the pond and transport it to the head of the waterfall via pipes or tubing.

A pump is the most important (and most expensive) piece of equipment you'll need for your waterfall. So don't just rush out and buy one—make sure you do a little homework first.

This is an example of a common water pump performance curve.

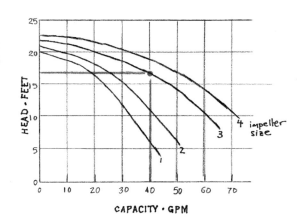

Part 1

The most important thing to understand is that it's harder for a pump to propel water through a vertical pipe than a horizontal one. Therefore, the number of gallons of water that your pump is able to circulate every hour will decrease in direct proportion to the height of your waterfall. The technical name for this is "head loss," and there are complicated mathematical formulas for figuring it out. Basically, all it means is that the taller your waterfall, the more powerful the pump you will need to get a sufficient flow of the water to the top of it.

Taking head loss into consideration, you should buy a pump that will produce 50 to 100 gallons per hour for every inch that your waterfall is wide. That means that if your waterfall is 12 inches wide, you'll need to pump about 600 gallons per hour to produce a delicate veil of water flowing back into your pond, and 1,200 gallons an hour for a bolder cascade. (If you use less than 50 gallons per inch, the water won't have enough force to do more than trickle over the edge; more than 100 gallons per inch and the current will be too strong, as well as noisy.) It's also worth noting that the more water that flows through your watercourse, the further it will project out over the edge of your weir as it falls.

Pumps usually come with a maximum flow rate on the box, indicated by a GPH (Gallons Per Hour) rating. But don't buy a pump based on the number on the box alone—you need to know the height range for which that rating is valid. Good manufacturers indicate the flow rate for a variety of heights (often indicated as "vertical lift"), which are measured from the surface of the water, not the bottom of the pond. Make sure the pump you're considering will be able to deliver enough water to your waterfall.

If you find all of this too confusing, as your pond dealer for help— he or she should be able to help you figure it out.

It doesn't hurt to buy a pump that's a little more powerful than the one you think you'll need; you can just install a "T" in the tubing and send some of the water to your waterfall while the rest goes right back to your pond. A "T" will also give you some flexibility, because if you decide later that you want a bolder (or gentler) flow through your waterfall, you can just adjust it at the valve.

One of the other decisions you'll have to make when it comes to pumps is whether to buy one specifically for your waterfall or to simply use the outflow from your pond filter. If you decide on the latter, you can hide the filter unit itself behind or inside of the waterfall, with the outflow hose directed into the header pool. Just make sure your filter is able to process enough water for a pleasing flow.

You also need to make sure the tubing you use for your pump is big enough, because if it's too narrow, the flow of water through it may be slowed. Kink-free flexible tubing is best, but you can also use PVC pipe. However, because it's rigid, you'll have to use fittings to go around any bends, which will lead to more head loss.

Part 1

One last note on pumps: When it comes time to place your pump it in your pond, position it at the opposite end of the pool from the waterfall. This will give you the best water circulation by drawing it from one end and returning it to the other.

Using Streams

A stream is really a waterfall that is almost horizontal. Instead of flowing over a series of terraces or a lip of rock, it courses along a waterway that slopes much more gradually–often so gradually that the slope is all but imperceptible. But that difference aside, many of the same things that apply to waterfalls apply to streams.

Getting Started

Before rushing out to dig a streambed for your water garden, think about how streams occur in nature. They aren't just straight chutes of water; they meander across the landscape, with the water carving its own bed out of the landscape over time. Streambeds are

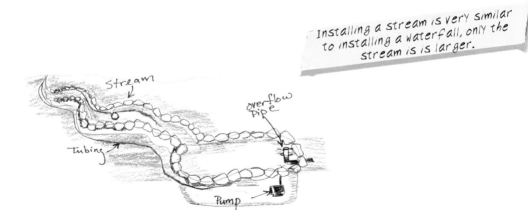

Installing a stream is very similar to installing a waterfall, only the stream is is larger.

rarely straight; because the water will be diverted by rocks and crevices that make up a natural part of the landscape. The more closely you can imitate this, the more natural your stream will look.

Start by studying the contours of your landscape. Then, sketch your stream on paper, including twists, turns, and small pools of water–perhaps even a bog garden, if you have the room.

When you're done, take your sketch outside and chart it out on the ground, using lime, spray paint, or string and stakes. Leave it for a couple of days and look at it from different angles. Does it look natural? Does the length and width seem proportionate to your pond? When you're satisfied that you have it right, it's time to dig.

The use of rocks will effectively create a natural stream-scape.

Slope and Width

Start digging at your pond and work your way toward the top of your stream. Keep in mind that the streambed should have a slight downhill slope; otherwise, the water will just sit there. A drop of 1 to 2 inches for every 10 feet of horizontal space should be about right. Start at the edge of your pond and work backward toward the head of your stream.

Start with a fairly narrow streambed–no more than a foot or two in width. If you make the streambed too wide, it won't fill completely and will look silly. You can always make the streambed wider later. You can also widen it slightly as it gets closer to the pond, which will make it look as if the stream is longer than it really is.

Because the width of a real stream varies at different points in the waterway, consider varying yours, too. In some places, for instance, broaden it out into small pools in a couple of places and grow plants in them, out of the path of the current. In all cases, make sure the edges of the streambed are level; if they're not, water will flow out of the lower side and onto your lawn or into your garden.

At the Start
If you want your stream to look natural, you need to make sure it begins out of sight–even if that just means that means hiding the starting point behind some bushes.

Alternatively, you can start with a small header pool, a basin where water from the outflow pipe collects before spilling down the streambed. The basin doesn't have to be fancy–an old milk jug or a bucket will do just fine. To make it look as if your stream is fed by a spring coming straight out of the ground, you can hide your pump outlet and header pool with heavy plantings, rocks, or logs.

Once you've excavated your streambed, spread a half-inch layer of sand on the sides and bottom to protect against rocks and twigs.

Part 1

Then it's time to line the streambed. You can buy pre-formed sections of pond that look like rock and come in both straight and curved sections, which you piece together to form a stream. But it's just as easy (and a lot less expensive) to use liner, and the end result is usually more natural looking.

If you have to piece sections of the liner together, start at the pond end of the stream and work backward, overlapping the upper section of liner over the lower one. Then glue each the two sections together using silicone adhesive. Make sure the liner extends over each side of the waterfall by at least a foot; if not, water may splash out of the stream and get under the liner. You can hide the edges of the liner with rock and overhanging plants.

Landscaping a Stream

This is the last step, and, for most people, the most fun. Use stones of different shapes and sizes, and arrange them randomly along the sides of the streambed. You can place some directly into the bed, too, to create interesting flow patterns. Many people also like to fill the bottom of their pond with gravel or pebbles; it not only makes the stream look more natural, it provides a place for the bacteria that make up your pond's biological

Multiple waterfalls can be built into large streams.

filter to grow. Dark-colored gravel usually looks more natural than light gravel.

Finally, put plants along the edges of the stream–just keep them out of the current itself, because most aquatic plants don't like moving water.

Special Considerations for Ponds

There are a couple of potential problems in adding a stream to your water garden. First, streams can hold a considerable amount of water, which is fine as long as your pump is running. However, if you turn it off, all the water in your stream will flow downhill to your pond, which is presumably already full, and the pond will overflow. To prevent this, consider installing an overflow pipe.

Not all streams appear natural; here, a formal channel directs overflow from a formal pond.

The other problem that can arise with ponds is essentially the reverse. If your streambed is dry because your pump has been off, turning it on again will cause the pump to draw water from your pond to refill it. If the volume of water contained by your stream is only about 10 or 20 percent of the total contained by your pond, you shouldn't have to worry–although your water level in the pond will

Part 1

This stream blends in perfectly with its surroundings, almost as if Mother Nature carved it there herself.

drop, it won't be so drastic as to stress fish or harm plants. However, if your streambed is very long, your pump could practically drain your pond in order to refill your stream. Therefore, you'll have to run the hose into your pond to replace the water that's being pumped out for your stream

A Note on Natural Streams

People who have natural streams crossing their property sometimes ask if they can divert the flow to supply their pond. The answer is that that's not always a good idea. Some municipalities have codes against doing this (check with your local water authority or agricultural department.) Even if there's no law against doing it, remember that diverting a natural stream could impact the ecology of the water both upstream and downstream. And equally important, anything that affects the water upstream will also affect your pond. If, for instance, pesticide-laden runoff from your neighbor's garden washes into the stream as it crosses his property, some of it is going to wind up in your pond, stressing or killing your fish.

Part Two

Garden Pond Styles and Types

by Jeffrey Kurtz

"I don't even want to know where you found both polka-dotted and striped plants-Your pond decorating privileges are over!"

Formal Water Garden Design

There are several common features of the formal water garden. First and foremost, symmetry and balance are hallmarks of the formal water garden. Designs typically conform to strict geometric shapes, such as circles, squares, rectangles and ovals. However, L-shapes, octagons and other configurations can be incorporated into

Formal water features, such as this pond, are useful for adding humidity to rooms in areas with dry climates.

Formal water gardens, such as this one in Switzerland, often require full-time gardeners.

formal pond design as well.

While there is no rule that says formal ponds must be placed in formal landscapes, they tend to have the best visual impact when situated among formally pruned planting beds with straight, balanced lines. (I'm thinking of carefully manicured hedges of boxwood or arborvitae with the occasional dwarf Alberta spruce topiary rather than natural-looking beds of perennials, herbaceous plants, and loosely pruned shrubs.)

Formal ponds are usually installed in close proximity to the home and complement the architecture and materials used in the construction of the house as well as any surrounding structures and "hardscaping"–patios, walls, walkways, and so on. Constructed of or incorporating materials such as concrete, brick, tile, cut stone, or stucco, formal ponds look decidedly man-made–and intentionally so.

Though many formal ponds have edges that are flush with the surrounding grade, low, raised walls are a common design element. This allows the attractive stones, bricks, tiles, or other building materials to be exhibited to their best advantage and provides a seat where the pond keeper can relax and "soak in" the fruits of his or her labor. Low walls also offer a certain measure of protection against accidental immersion for small children and people with limited mobility (e.g., wheelchair users).

One important note: If you live in an area with cold, harsh winters and choose to construct your pond out of concrete, it's highly recommended that you get a qualified contractor involved in the project. Concrete has a tendency to flake or crack due to the freezing and thawing cycles typical of northern climes, but a knowledgeable contractor will have the skills necessary to sidestep this problem. Hiring a professional contractor might cost you more at the outset of the project, but it will save you the price of costly repairs in the future–not to mention the frustration of watching your efforts crumble before your eyes.

Formal garden ponds frequently have classical statuary, water fountains, or combinations thereof as focal points. Nighttime illumination can be employed on these features to create a dramatic interplay of light, water movement, architecture, and shadow. Of course, accents are also provided within the pond through the strategic, symmetrical placement of water plants and around the edges of the pond with decorative containers planted with coordinating annual and perennial flowers.

The Formal Pond on an Informal Budget

With all this talk about raised stonewalls, statuary, fountains, and

Swimming pools make excellent formal water gardens that can house koi and other pond fishes.

professional contractors, it may sound as if the formal pond is well beyond the average homeowner's financial means. However, this is not necessarily true. While a formal pond can get costly, even the most frugal pond fancier can enjoy at least a taste of formality by incorporating a water feature with formal flair into the landscape. A setup as simple as a concrete urn or decorative ceramic planter filled with water and adorned with a single dwarf water lily (or, perhaps, one marginal plant and a few floating plants) can make quite a statement in the right setting. Cluster several water-filled vessels of varying heights together on a patio or deck, and you've added another intriguing dimension.

A classical-themed concrete fountain, available at just about any home-and-garden retailer, can be dressed up with several floating water hyacinths, providing the soothing sound of trickling water, the delicate-yet-ephemeral beauty of the hyacinth blooms, and the formal character of the fountain itself–all for the minimal investment of a few hundred dollars.

If you're a little more ambitious, it's possible to create a larger formal-style pond using readily available–and relatively inexpensive–landscaping materials. Several landscaping timbers can be stacked in alternating fashion and lined with a sheet of PVC to create a rectangular pool. Simply use whole lengths for the longer sides and half-lengths for the shorter ends. Iron rebar rods can be inserted through predrilled holes at the corners to reinforce the walls. Some companies even manufacture special interlocking timbers complete with wooden pegs that can be used for this purpose. If you're really creative, you can use this type of system to create multiple tiers and work in some nice finishing touches, such as corner benches and planters.

Prefabricated concrete blocks–the kind sold at garden centers for building retaining walls and raised planting beds–can also be used to create attractive raised ponds with a formal flair. While they're somewhat more costly than landscape timbers, they are available in a wide variety of styles and colors and will allow you more freedom when it comes to the shape of your pond, including circles and ovals with tapering walls.

Examples of Fine Formal Water Gardens

While an exhaustive discussion of formal water garden design is beyond the scope of this book, there are several common designs worth exploring in a little more detail.

The Formal Pool

The first of these is the formal pool. Typically round, square, or rectangular in shape (though some delightfully intricate variations

Formal garden ponds usually contain at least one other formal feature, such as a water fountain as shown here.

exist), the formal pool can be either sunken or raised and may be used to create an enchanting focal point in a courtyard garden, a pleasing diversion on a garden pathway—for example, where two cobblestone pathways intersect—or for visual impact on a patio or terrace.

Floating and emergent plants are used minimally or restricted to a few dramatic specimens in the formal pool, and the water is kept still in order to mirror the surrounding architecture or plantings and the sky overhead. Submerged oxygenating plants may be utilized to help clarify the water. The edges of sunken formal pools can be softened with plantings of pachysandra, English ivy, myrtle, or other groundcovers.

The Formal Fountain

Building on the design of the formal pool is the formal fountain. There are endless variations on this theme, but the design usually consists of a round or square pool with low, raised walls and a statuary fountain focal point. A jet fountain produced by a submerged pump may be used as an alternative to (or in combination with) the

Part 2

statue fountain. A plethora of pump attachments is available to create dramatic effects with the water jet, including single vertical jets, dome or mushroom shapes, water arches, a fleur-de-lis pattern, and just about any other water design you can think of.

The design elements of the formal fountain can be as simple or elaborate as the imagination allows, ranging from the minimalist to the obscenely opulent, but, true to the formal style, the building materials will usually mirror that of the surrounding architecture.

Formal water fountains may have many tiers.

Part 2

Formal Waterfalls

One of the most intriguing formal water features is the waterfall. Unlike natural waterfalls, formal waterfalls typically don't meander along a winding streambed, bounce off rocks, and spill randomly into an informal pool. Rather, the water cascades in uniform sheets over formal water steps or sills, creating a most pleasing musical and visual impression, into a formal pool or canal. The soothing interplay of clean, symmetrical lines and crystal-clear curtains of water is the desired element here.

Part 2

Formal waterfalls are usually very unique and quite pleasing to the eye.

The possibilities for creating impressive formal falls are limited only by the imagination (and, perhaps, the pocketbook). One popular and very striking motif is the use of water stair-steps to flank a garden pathway or to l ink formal terraces. Depending on the materials used in construction, stair-step falls can assume a sleek, contemporary look or a classical aspect. If something less dramatic is preferred, a simple water trough pouring a glistening sheet of water into a large catch basin can breathe new life into a garden, courtyard or home entryway.

If you've incorporated koi or other fish into your water garden design, a waterfall has a practical side as well. As the water cascades into your formal pool, it brings much-needed oxygen into the pool for the benefit of the fish.

Statuary in the Formal Water Garden

As I mentioned previously, statuary, whether plumbed as a fountain or freestanding, is a common feature of the formal water garden. And never before have pond keepers had so many statuary options to choose from, in so many colors and finishes, for such reasonable prices! Visit any home-and-garden retailer or water garden-supply store, and you'll see what I mean.

Choosing statues or statuary fountains is one of the more fun aspects of creating a pond–sort of the "icing on the cake" after you've dealt with all the practical details of construction. It's also at this point that you really get to work your own personality into the project.

So what sort of statement would you like your pond to make? Classical? Religious? Sentimental? Comical? Sure, dignified themes are commonplace in formal water gardens, but that doesn't mean your pond can't convey a sense of humor. There's always room for a little mischief!

All of the themes I've described above (and more) are available nowadays. In the classical vein, you can choose from Venus de Milo, Bacchus, the four seasons, adorable-yet-tacky tinkling cherubs, and just about every other mythological figure you can imagine. Choose from Jesus, the Holy Family, angels, St. Francis and Buddha, to

Formal water features often include statues that spit water into a basin, where it is then pumped back through the statue.

name but a few, for a religious theme. Want to go Medieval on your formal water garden? Work in some grotesques and gargoyles. If sentimental is more your speed, you can always incorporate the ubiquitous Boy and Girl Beneath Umbrella statue. I've seen gnome statues and fountains for sale as well, but putting these in a formal pond setting may be "pushing the envelope" a little.

The point is, there's virtually no limit to your statuary options. Just be sure that the style and color scheme complement, rather than detract from, the overall theme of your water garden.

Another important axiom to keep in mind when shopping for statuary is, "less is more." You don't want to overwhelm the composition or undermine the symmetry of your water garden by cluttering it with too many concrete figures.

The Freestanding Fountain

If you don't have the space or budget to accommodate a formal water garden *and* a statuary fountain, you can always purchase a simple freestanding fountain with a formal design. Though freestanding fountains come in all shapes and sizes, most are very similar from the standpoint of setup and operation.

The typical design consists of a pedestal, catch basin, water pump and plastic tubing, collar, and plumbed statue. The basin is placed on top of the pedestal and the water pump sets in the middle of the basin. The power cord for the pump runs through a hole in the basin and down through the pedestal. A short, threaded PVC pipe fits in the basin hole to prevent the water from running out. Both the water pump and PVC pipe are concealed beneath the collar, which is then topped with the statue. The pump connects via plastic tubing to a metal tube at the bottom of the statue, which ultimately carries the water to the fountain opening, where it trickles down to the catch basin. For fountains with more than one tier, additional basins and collars are included in the package.

Freestanding fountains are gaining popularity among those who wish to add flair to their formal garden ponds.

Part 2

Be sure to site your fountain on level ground, or you'll have trouble keeping the water from overflowing on one side, especially on windy days. Also, depending on the size of your water pump, you may need to use a restrictor clamp (usually included with the pump) on the plastic tubing to keep water from shooting out of the fountain opening in a powerful stream. Of course, be sure that the electrical connection to the water pump is properly installed and rated for outdoor use.

Other Ornaments and Accents for Formal Water Gardens

Along with statuary and fountains, there are a wide variety of ornaments, accents, and accessories for garden ponds. The challenge, however, with choosing accessories for the formal water garden is selecting items that complement the overall theme and symmetry of design and don't make your formal water feature seem too, well, informal. So what are your options?

Floating Ornaments

A popular trend in water garden accents is the floating ornament. For example, if you like the look of water lilies but don't want to fool around with the real thing, you can buy floating, artificial water lilies (pads and blooms sold separately). Various floating aquatic critters, such as frogs, turtles, salamanders, hippos, snails, and crocodiles are also available. Some floating critters have been designed to sit on top of the floating lily pads. If tastefully done, these ornaments can enhance the overall impression of your pond. Overdo it, though, and your formal pond will lose its cohesiveness.

Spouting Ornaments

Don't have the space for a tiered fountain or fountain statue? A smaller, decorative spouting ornament might just fit the bill. Usually shaped like aquatic creatures—fish, turtles, frogs, and such— or small classical figurines (more diminutive than the average plumbed statue), spouting ornaments can add just the right measure of water movement and whimsy. Again, take care to select spouting ornaments with a style and finish that complement your formal water feature, and don't overdo it.

Pond Lighting

One of the most exciting trends in pond accessories today is low-voltage pond lighting. Tasteful lighting can make even the most understated pond appear spectacular after sundown. Submersible halogen lamps highlight every bubble, splash, and shimmer to great

Spitting frogs seem to be one of the more popular "spitting" ornaments.

effect and exaggerate the water's lucidity. For a touch of romance, add colored lenses to your underwater fixtures. You can change the colors whenever you like to suit your mood.

Fanciful floating surface lights, in the shape of water lilies, aquatic animals, or globes, are yet another intriguing element. These are fun conversation starters when entertaining guests outdoors, and there are enough styles available to suit every taste. However, try to avoid mixing surface lights with underwater lights. Otherwise, the visual effect may become muddled.

Aboveground landscape lights can even be utilized in pond illumination. Directing them toward fountains, falls, or other prominent features can really bring them to life after hours. Just take care to

Part 2

Water and electricity are a deadly combination, it's a good idea to get a qualified electrician involved in the installation of Your pond lighting.

avoid flooding your water feature with excessive illumination. Remember, subtlety is the key to effective pond lighting. For a consistent nighttime display, you might want to connect your pond lights to an electronic timer, which will turn them on at the same time every evening or, if a photo sensor is incorporated in the timer's design, in response to reduced light levels.

Informal Water Garden Design

Whereas formal pond design emphasizes symmetry, straight lines and architectural cohesiveness, the informal pond is characterized by natural, flowing curves and is designed to blend in to a garden setting unobtrusively. While the formal pond celebrates man-made structure and features plants and fish only minimally, the informal

Informal water gardens are often quite large and provide you with the freedom to be creative.

pond attempts to conceal the traces of construction and to recreate nature through the copious use of aquatic plants as well as fish and the wildlife that is naturally drawn to a pond setting (frogs, toads, butterflies, dragonflies, birds, thirsty mammals, etc.).

It's the Natural Thing to Do

Because informal ponds are intended to merge with their surroundings, existing landscape features, such as large boulders, sloping hills, or mass plantings, are often incorporated into their design. After all, it 's easier to make your pond conform to the style and contour of your existing landscape rather than the other way around. Fountains are usually left out of informal pond designs (the big, classical-style kind, anyway), but small waterfalls or streams are commonly utilized to introduce the soothing timbre of trickling water and to enhance the overall visual impression.

Informal water gardens are often blended with outdoor scenery to look as if they have always been there.

Plastic pond-liner edges and other unnatural features can be concealed with natural materials, such as mulch, fieldstone, or river rock. Better yet, they can be softened with strategic plantings of groundcover, perennials, and low-growing shrubs. Spreading junipers, recumbent yews, cotoneaster, azaleas, *Hosta*, astilbe, bleeding heart,

English ivy, pachysandra, myrtle and even laceleaf Japanese maples are just a small sampling of plants that are appropriate for softening the edges of a pond.

Ironically, it can be a greater challenge to create a completely natural-looking pond than to achieve a strictly formal pond design. That's because artifice, as you might imagine, tends to stand out like a sore thumb in a natural setting. One common mistake that leaves a natural pond looking decidedly unnatural is to ring the entire perimeter with nothing more than a single row of fieldstone, thereby creating a contrived "string-of-pearls" look.

The Finer Points of Informal Ponds

The informal pond is, perhaps, the most popular form of water garden with homeowners for a variety of reasons. Informal design can work in a broader range of garden settings, and it provides greater opportunities for creativity–especially with water plant color, texture, and arrangement. Also, informal ponds tend to be less expensive to build relative to their formal counterparts, and they're generally easier to undertake as a first garden pond project. Best of all, they can turn just about any garden setting, regardless of its size, into a tranquil retreat from the hustle and bustle of 21st century living.

An informal pond can be as large or as small as the homeowner's budget allows. However, in order to produce the best visual impression and the most enjoyment out of your pond, it's essential that the size of your pond is in proportion to the size of your yard. You don't want your pond to be so large that it overwhelms your landscape or so small that it gets lost visually.

Practical Solutions to Creating Informal Water Gardens

There are numerous ways to arrive at a very satisfactory informal water feature. How you decide to approach it depends on how large you want the pond to be, how much effort you want to put forth in the project, and how much money you want to part with. To a certain extent, the larger the pond, the greater the effort–and the greater the cash investment. However, with the materials available for building ponds today, you can have just about any size pond for a very modest price. Let's start with the smallest and work our way up.

Whiskey barrels are rustic in appearance.

The Whiskey Barrel Water Garden

Most gardeners are familiar with the half-whiskey-barrel planter, but did you know this old garden standby could double as a quaint informal water feature? The rustic character of these planters makes them ideal for small garden, patio, deck or balcony settings. Simply line the barrel with a sheet of flexible liner (or one of the rigid plastic liners designed for just such a purpose), fill it with water, drop in a

few water plants, add a few fish, and you're in the pond business–
well, on a really small scale, anyway.

Why is a liner necessary for a vessel designed to contain liquid, you
ask? Residual alcohol and toxic tannic acid from the oak used in the
construction of whiskey barrels could leach into the water to the
detriment of your fish and plants if you don't use a liner or, at the
very least, a polyurethane or multi-surface sealer.

The biggest drawback to the whiskey barrel garden is that over the
course of several gardening seasons, the metal rings that surround
the barrel tend to rust and slide down, causing the barrel slats to fall
apart and leaving you with a sloppy mess. This can be avoided by
simply replacing the barrel from time to time. They're not costly,
and you can find them at just about any garden center.

Don't care for the look of a whiskey barrel but still want a
diminutive informal water feature? You can achieve a similar effect
with a large clay pot–again, sealed on the inside with polyurethane
or a multi-surface sealer. Without the sealer, the water will
continually weep through the pot. Also, be sure to close off the
drainage hole at the bottom of the pot (if one is present), using
plumber's epoxy or aquarium-grade silicone sealant.

The Sunken Preformed Pond

Moving up in pond size, we come to the sunken preformed pond.
This popular form of water feature is created by installing a

Part 2

Part 2

a Preformed pond liners can usually be worked into a landscape quite effectively.

preformed pond liner made of rigid plastic or fiberglass into the ground. These liners are sold at virtually every water garden retailer and home-and-garden store, and most have a pleasant meandering shape that is just right for building an informal pond–although round, oval and kidney-shaped liners are available, too. Some liners can be surprisingly sophisticated, with built-in waterfall features or multiple compartments. Preformed liners range in water capacity from under 50 gallons to around 200 gallons. However, the larger sizes can get surprisingly expensive.

The rigid pond liner takes the guesswork out of pond design because what you see is what you get. They're also relatively easy to install. You simply dig a hole that matches the contour of the liner and set it in place. And, because these liners are relatively difficult to puncture, you don't have to be overly concerned about leaks. Nonetheless, it's still a wise move to install about a 6-inch sand underlay beneath the liner before you install it to protect the plastic or fiberglass from the sharp edges of rocks in the soil underneath. Even a rigid liner can be penetrated over time due to the weight of the water pressing against sharp surfaces.

Another advantage to preformed ponds is that shelves are often incorporated in the design of the medium to large-sized models so various marginal plants and water lilies can be placed at just the appropriate depth. Also, the liner edges are fairly inconspicuous and easy to conceal or soften with terrestrial plants and other natural materials.

On the downside, preformed pond liners do not allow a great deal of design flexibility. As I mentioned, what you see is what you get, so you can't alter the shape of your pond if the natural layout or contours of your landscape call for it. Lack of depth can also be a negative with rigid pond liners. Most are extremely shallow and, therefore, very limiting from the standpoint of keeping fish alive in the pond during the winter in colder areas. Also, if your goal is to construct a slightly larger water feature, say a very modest 10 x 15 feet pond, you're not likely to find a rigid liner big enough to suit your purposes.

Staying Flexible

For building larger informal ponds, nothing beats the flexible pond liner. Go flexible, and the sky is the limit when it comes to the layout of your pond. You can make it as deep as want—which, if you plan to keep a school of koi, becomes something of a necessity rather than a luxury. You're also not limited in the number and depths of shelves that you can include in your pond design, which gives you more freedom to include a greater diversity of water plants. Perhaps most important, a flexible liner will give you the

Part 2

most, well, flexibility when it comes to working your water feature seamlessly into a natural landscape design.

Several types of flexible liner are available to pond enthusiasts, including (but not limited to) PVC, ethylene-propylene, and butyl rubber. Each of these options has its advantages and disadvantages for pond applications, but, arguably, the best choice is ethylene-propylene, more specifically EPDM (Ethylene-Propylene-Diene-Monomer). This material is designed to endure for up to 20 years, is more flexible than PVC and, hence, easier to install, and is best suited for use in colder climates. The only downside to EPDM is its higher price tag, but when you factor in its superior reliability and workability, the added cost becomes less significant.

Pond liners allow you to have the most design and style flexibility.

The one major drawback to flexible liners versus rigid preformed liners is the greater propensity for accidentally puncturing the material. Care must be taken to avoid using sharp rocks or other sharp objects in the design that could tear the liner and leave your hopes and dreams high and dry. It's critical with flexible liners, even more so than with rigid preformed liners, to put down a 6-inch sand underlay prior to installation.

Making Connections: The Informal Garden Stream

The informal equivalent to the formal rill is the re-circulating garden stream. This delightful water feature borrows from and blends in with the surrounding natural environment and is a great way to introduce the soothing sound of running water–a sound that proves irresistible to both people and wildlife. Besides, building a modest re-circulating stream can be a really fun project for the entire family.

Before we begin to explore the garden stream, let me add this one caveat: If this is your first foray into pond keeping, you might want to consider "getting your feet wet" with a single pond first. Once you've mastered that, you can add a second pond and connect the two with a streambed. Also, careful planning is key to success with a project such as this. Not only will you avoid the pitfalls of purchasing materials in inadequate or excessive amounts, but you'll also be much happier in the long run with the design of a carefully planned stream.

Informal garden streams are always fascinating to build and watch.

To create your informal garden stream, you'll need a gently sloping area; two preformed pond liners, one approximately 50 gallons in capacity and the other approximately 200 gallons (or, if you prefer, an adequate amount of flexible pond liner); the appropriate length of flexible liner to function as a streambed; sand to use as an underlay for your liners; a water pump rated between 100 and 200 gallons per hour; a return hose with all necessary connections; flat rocks and river rocks to naturalize your streambed; an electrical connection for the pump; and, of course, plants–shrubs, perennials, groundcovers, and so on–to blend your stream into the landscape.

Install the smaller pond upstream and the larger pond downstream, making sure they are level. Dig out the streambed, ensuring a minimum depth of around 4 inches and a minimum bottom width of 6 inches. The banks should be sloping. For added interest, consider digging a small shelf to function as a waterfall.

Next, install your streambed liner, overlapping lengths if necessary to avoid leaks. Conceal the liner edges and naturalize the streambed with flat rocks and river rock.

Install the pump in the lower pond, and run the return hose to the upper pond, burying the hose in a shallow trough along the edge of the stream. The services of a qualified electrician should be called upon for the installation of the pump's electrical supply.

Once everything is in place and before adding any substantial ornamentation, fill the ponds with water, fire up the pump, and test the flow of the stream. When you're satisfied that everything is working properly, you can begin to naturalize the stream with plants and work in any other decorative features or ornaments that you desire.

Of course, this is necessarily a very rudimentary description of the installation process. Before digging a single shovel full of soil, it's a wise idea to consult with a pond professional. You can also find step-by-step instructions for building a garden stream in numerous water gardening books and on a variety of Internet sites.

Accents and Ornaments for the Informal Water Garden

All of the ornaments, accents, and statuary that were discussed in the chapter on formal water gardens are also available for use in informal water gardens. But in keeping with the naturalistic character of the informal pond, formal accents, such as classical statuary, formal fountains, and grandiose lighting schemes, are generally eschewed in favor of more naturalistic or rustic elements.

Surprising Statues and Natural Sculpture

Statues are best used sparingly in the informal pond. For best effect, tuck them away among foliage and other natural elements so they appear as pleasant "surprises" rather than prominent features. Semi-submerged or spouting wildlife statues, fish, frogs, turtles, crocodiles, hippos and so on, seem to work well as do whimsical or sentimental statues when used in moderation. One of my favorite statuary motifs is the statue of a child or cherub sitting on the edge of the pond, feet dangling over the bank, gazing wistfully into the water.

Bird statues such as these herons act as scarecrows to protect against real herons from coming in and eating your fish.

Unique sculpture that draws on natural themes and natural materials–and even some abstract or surreal artwork–can seem "at home" in the informal water garden and, at the same time, lend a sense of individuality to the space without seeming artificial.

For The Birds

Birdbaths, partially obscured among plantings, are a nice finishing touch, not to mention another source of refreshment for the numerous winged beauties that will soon hone in on your water feature. And while you're giving the birds a place to drink and bathe, why not give them something to eat as well? A well-stocked birdfeeder, located in the vicinity of your informal pond, will ensure a steady supply of these feathered songsters. When installing a birdfeeder, however, make sure that it is not located too close to thick plantings or heavy brush where cats can conceal themselves to launch an attack.

Informal Benches and Decks

A very welcome feature around the informal pond is the garden bench. What better place to spend a few peaceful moments, taking in all the sights, sounds, and fragrances of your water garden?

Though the classical-style concrete bench (you know, the one every garden center sells with the Ionic volutes on the support pedestals) might not blend well with your informal water feature, unpretentious concrete or stone benches or country-style ones made of wood or bent twigs will fit in just fine.

aWooden porches or decks can be effective viewing platforms for large informal water gardens.

Part 2

A wooden deck built across one end or along one edge of the pond is another welcome feature in the informal water garden. A deck offers another opportunity for the pond keeper to enjoy his or her handiwork at close range–as well as a place to do a little foot dangling just like that statue I mentioned earlier. A deck can also create the dramatic visual impression that it bridges the pond–i.e., the water flows beneath and beyond the deck–even though it doesn't. Strategic use of marginal plants and terrestrial plants beyond the deck can help to complete the illusion.

Lighting Nature's Way

Submerged or floating electric lights don't have much of a place in the informal water garden. Rely instead on the effect of natural sunlight on moving water and the reflection of natural light–from sun, moon and stars–off of the surface of the pond. If artificial lighting is to be used at all, it should mimic the quality of natural light sources rather than provide dramatic manmade effects.

Keep it Real

Floating wildlife and water lily ornaments are well suited for the informal water garden setting. Just take care to avoid overwhelming the real things with artificial ones. In general, as you consider which ornaments, statues, or accents to choose, keep in mind that artifice is generally considered something to be avoided or used only sparingly in the informal pond. After all, you don't want to end up with something that appears to be integrated with nature–not a water feature on a miniature golf course.

Color in the Water Garden

When most people think about color in the water garden, or any type of garden for that matter, the first thing that comes to mind is bloom color. While the color of flowers plays an important part in water gardening, especially with the myriad of water lily cultivars that are now available to pond keepers, the color and texture of foliage

Water hyacinths are striking when they blossom into a field of purple flowers.

plays an even bigger role.

In the water garden, visual interest depends largely on creating attractive and complementary foliage combinations. From the heart-shaped pads of water lilies, to the glossy leaves and bulbous air-filled bladders of water hyacinth, to the sword-like foliage of water irises, to the arrow-shaped leaves of the American arrowhead, to the broad, tropical-looking foliage of the various canna hybrids, shape and texture must combine in a pleasing visual effect.

Terrestrial shade gardens offer an interesting parallel to this rule. While some shade-loving plants, such as the ever-popular azaleas and rhododendrons, put on quite a spectacular floral display in spring, foliage is "king" in the shade garden. Plants such as *Hosta*, ferns, hydrangeas, boxwood, holly, viburnum, and, of course, azaleas and rhododendrons come together to create a charming, serene impression. Flowers are a nice touch, but the terrestrial shade garden doesn't depend on them–nor does the water garden.

The Many Moods of Color

Color, provided either by flowers or foliage, affects the theme or impression of a water garden in many ways. Depending on which colors you choose to include, your water feature will either have a calm, soothing effect or a cheerful, lively effect. For example, cool colors, such as the blues, whites, and soft pastels, tend to recede visually. This produces a more serene, meditative impression when

Part 2

viewed. Because they recede, cool colors also tend to make a pond appear larger.

The water iris (*Iris laevigata*) with its beardless blue flowers and soft-green leaves; the water hyacinth (*Eichhornia crassipes*) with its delicate light-blue flowers; and the water lily cultivars *Nymphaea* 'Blue Beauty,' *Nymphaea xmarliacea* 'Carnea' (light pink flowers), and *N.* 'Gonnere' (white flowers) are just a sampling of water plants with cool-colored blooms.

Warm colors, such as reds, yellows, and oranges, on the other hand, tend to advance visually, creating a more dramatic, exciting impression. They also have the effect of making a pond appear smaller. Some choices of plants with warm, vibrant colors include *Canna* 'Bengal Tiger' with its yellow-striped leaves and bright-orange flowers, cardinal flower (*Lobelia cardinalis*) with its bright-red flowers, *Crocosmia* 'Lucifer' with its flame-red flowers, and the water lily cultivars *Nymphaea* 'Mayla' (rich fuchsia blooms) and 'Vesuve' (brilliant-red flowers).

Another tool you can use to help you select plants that harmonize

An informal pond such as this are what dreams are made of.

chromatically is the good old-fashioned color wheel. If you remember the color wheel from your high school art classes, you'll recall that colors immediately adjacent to each other match nicely because they have a pigment in common. Colors directly opposite one another, for example, orange and blue, are considered complementary colors and contrast nicely (yes, believe it or not, orange and blue flowers are quite striking together). The color wheel is limited somewhat, however, by the countless subtle variations in hue that exist in plants.

Plant Color in the Formal Water Garden

Because symmetry of form and cohesiveness of composition are so important in formal pond design, a "riot" of color and texture produced by mass plantings is an unwelcome sight. In the formal garden, water plants are often restricted to one impressive specimen, such as an umbrella plant (*Cyperus alternifolius* 'Gracilis'), or a single stand of plants in order to avoid overwhelming the design. Also, if the focal point of a formal pond happens to be a prominent water feature, such as a fountain or water jet, you certainly wouldn't want to distract the eye from that feature by cluttering up the scene with too many plants.

Plant Color in the Informal Water Garden

Though your options for including plant color increase considerably with informal water gardens, cohesiveness of theme still counts. If you have a pond with tranquil, cool colors, you don't want it to transition into a landscape that features vibrant, eye-catching colors–or vice versa. On the contrary, the color scheme of your aquatic plants should coalesce with that of the marginals, the terrestrial plants located just above the water line, and the plants in the surrounding landscape. That means some restraint in plant selection is required even with the most informal water garden.

Color can make the difference between a "nice" water garden and a "fantastic" water garden.

Given the role terrestrial plants play in informal water garden design, it stands to reason that pond keepers will benefit considerably from learning about the different terrestrial perennials, groundcovers, shrubs, and even small trees that will harmonize with their pond plants. It's an ongoing learning process that can start with a trip to your local nursery or water garden center.

The Water Lily: Water Garden Color Workhorse

From tiny water-filled containers to medium-sized pools to sprawling ponds, you can't beat the water lilies, *Nymphaea* spp., when it comes to introducing floral color to a water garden. With a seemingly endless variety of cultivars on the market representing just about every size and color shade imaginable; the water lilies are, perhaps, the most versatile and adaptable of all the aquatic plants.

Water lilies are always lovely in full bloom.

Set against an attractive canvas of upright marginals (sedges, rushes, cattails, etc.), which are typically planted at the edge of the water feature opposite the usual vantage point, water lilies really come into their own. Some are exceptionally fragrant as well as strikingly beautiful. There are even fragrant night-blooming varieties that will add perfume and subtle color to an evening stroll around the pond.

Perhaps the only drawback to the water lilies is that there are just so darn many of them that the pond keeper may be tempted to mix in too many different cultivars, thereby compromising the water garden's color theme.

Accents and Ornaments

Various water garden ornaments and accents can be used to bring in a splash of color when the plants aren't cooperating by blooming. For example, painted fountains or statues can provide a hint of color–though usually in subtle, muted tones. Ceramic planters with polychromatic or Oriental designs can really add a touch of elegance. For a considerably bolder color statement, you can experiment with submerged lighting outfitted with colored lenses or colored floodlights directed toward a prominent water feature or statue. However, as you might imagine, this approach is best suited to the formal water garden. Colored glass vessels of various shape and character make a really interesting statement around water gardens with a modern flair.

Along with these suggestions, there are limitless other opportunities for incorporating color through decorative elements. Just be sure that the artwork and ornaments you choose complement, rather than compete with, your water garden theme.

Colorful Koi

Of course, one of the most interesting and pleasurable ways to introduce color to a water feature is through the addition of Japanese koi. The intensity of koi color combinations has got to be seen in order to be believed—and it's always on the move as these regal fish fin their way around the pond. Sound interesting? Then read on to the next chapter where we will discuss koi in greater detail.

If you'd rather not make the comparatively sizeable investment for a fish that could end up

Large koi need deep water and special requirements to grow properly, so be sure to build your pond for koi from the start.

Part 2

Koi like this Grand Champion Kohaku may cost several thousands of dollars.

as a snack for a hungry heron, fancy goldfish can be a nice compromise. While they may not exhibit the same stunning color combinations as koi, they're quite attractive in their own right, and they're very inexpensive.

Part 2

The Oriental Water Garden

In these chaotic, fast-paced times, pond keepers strive to create a small oasis of tranquility with their water gardens. Whereas most ponds provide at least some degree of quietude for the world-weary, the oriental water garden elevates this attribute to an art form.

The Oriental water garden

The lush greenery, crystal clear water, and prize-winning koi make this pond one of Japan's finest.

combines three essential elements–water, stone, and plants–to produce a serene environment that is conducive to a meditative state. Typically positioned so that the garden appears to be a natural extension of the distant landscape, natural surroundings are painstakingly replicated in miniature. Pools, water-filled vessels, and garden streams represent natural lakes and rivers. Boulders, mounded rocks, and carefully manicured shrubs suggest mountains. Forests are recreated with stands of upright marginal water plants and perennials. Large stones and masses of water plants become islands.

Chinese and Japanese Influences

I should point out that using the term "Oriental water garden" to describe a particular theme of water feature is a bit misleading. There are both Chinese and Japanese interpretations of the water garden, and both contribute something quite distinct to the art of pond keeping.

Bridges are very popular features in Japanese-style water gardens.

In the Chinese tradition, elaborate rockwork, courtyards, pavilions, and bridges impart a very architectural character. Plants are used sparingly, and those that are included in the design tend to have symbolic significance. Intricate pathways leading through the garden and bridges crossing over water features are intended to represent life's journeys–an effect often lost on Americans who tend not to think in symbolic terms.

Japanese water gardens, with their serene reflecting pools, artfully placed rocks, and traditional stone lanterns, are somewhat more familiar to American water gardeners. The three essential elements–water, stone, and plants–are included in relatively equal measure, which is, perhaps, more appealing to American sensibilities. In the Japanese garden, water creates a contemplative mood through its sound, motion and reflective properties.

A Water Feature Without the Water

An intriguing variation on a water feature that commonly appears in Japanese gardens is the traditional Zen gravel garden. Consisting of uniform-sized gravel that is raked and cleaned of debris meticulously, the Zen garden is intended to create a state of tranquility for the viewer.

The raked gravel represents a large body of water, i.e., the ocean, and the lines left behind by the stout-tined rake represent waves moving over the sea. Boulders and larger rocks placed around the gravel garden replicate islands, and the gravel around the rocks is raked to appear as waves breaking on the shore. It's a

Asian Influence

The distinction between Chinese and Japanese water gardens has largely been blurred for Westerners who often borrow elements of each style with joyful abandon.

fascinating "water feature" that doesn't have a drop of water in it!

Because many of the traditions behind Oriental garden elements are poorly understood, it's not uncommon for oriental-style water gardens to become a bit incoherent. Careful forethought, plenty of preplanning, and a little research are all key to avoiding a contrived look.

Ornaments and Accents for the Oriental Water Garden

Given the unpretentious, naturalistic character of the Oriental water garden, any manmade ornaments or accents that you choose to include should be few in number, consist of natural materials (or, at least, have the appearance of being made of natural materials), and harmonize with the design of your water garden.

Statuary is very important in Japanese water gardens.

For example, the traditional bamboo fountain is always welcome. If you're not familiar with this fountain, it's very simple in construction, consisting of little more than a vertical section of bamboo that joins with a horizontal spout. The water trickles from the spout into a stone basin or into a pond, creating a most delightful, soothing, natural music. A variation on this simple design creates a rhythmic knocking as the water pours out, which is designed to frighten deer–and their insatiable appetites for ornamental plants–away from the garden.

Of course, an Oriental water garden just isn't an Oriental water garden without the traditional stone lantern. Stone lanterns range in size from the very tiny to the towering, so the challenge becomes matching the size of your lantern to the size of your pond without one overwhelming the other. If the cost of stone is prohibitive, you can always go with a natural-tone concrete version instead.

Statues and statuary fountains can work, but you have to be discriminating about the design. Elegant, curvilinear statues or fountains of cranes, for example, have just the right quality and symbolic value for the oriental water garden. On the other hand, a soaring concrete knock-off of Michelangelo's "David" spouting water from its mouth might not seem quite "at home."

A simple stone bridge spanning a calm reflecting pool brings the water gardener into closer contact with his handiwork, and an unadorned stone bench at the pool's edge provides the perfect spot for relaxation and quiet meditation. Natural steppingstones can be used to lead visitors from one scenic vista to the next and, perhaps, across the pond shallows.

If the house is immediately adjacent to the water garden, a rain chain connected to the eaves makes an enchanting impression. A rain chain is a decorative-yet-functional watercourse that funnels

Part 2

Delicate oriental wind chimes evoke a contemplative mood and harmonize well with gently trickling water features. Temple bells add another appealing musical note that, although manmade, is in keeping with the simple, serene environment of the Oriental garden.

rainwater from the roof of a home into a collection vessel on the ground. The funnels, which are linked together in a long vertical chain (hence the name), are often shaped like flowers or other natural objects that fit nicely into the Japanese garden setting. These beautiful chains have adorned homes and temples in Japan for centuries.

Of course, this is just a small sampling of the ornaments and accents that you can choose from. Just remember when picking out accessories for the Oriental water garden that simplicity is preferable to sophistication and artlessness is desired over artifice.

The Koi Pond

One of the most significant contributions of the Japanese water gardening tradition to the art of pond keeping is the koi pond. Koi are brilliantly colorful relatives of the common carp (*Cyprinus carpio*) that can turn an already stunning pond into something truly spectacular.

Koi, or nishikigoi, as they're called in Japan, were first bred approximately 200 years ago. Since that time, 14 spectacular color varieties and numerous subdivisions of those varieties have been developed. The Japanese names used to categorize these wonderful fish can leave you rather tongue-tied and scratching your head at first, but they're not quite as complicated as they might seem once your able to "put the name to a face," so to speak.

For example, a kohaku koi is a white fish with red markings, a taisho sanke is white with red and black markings, utsurimono koi are black and white, and so on. Each variety is then subdivided into groups of fish that have the same color combinations but in different patterns. Of course, this is an oversimplification that will have koi purists gritting their teeth, but you get the idea.

This is a fine example of the kohaku koi.

Part 2

One interesting note about koi: Unlike the various tropical fish we keep in aquariums with glass or acrylic walls, koi are exclusively pond fish and, so, are bred to be most attractive when viewed from above. Somehow, koi kept within the confines of a glass aquarium seem like (excuse the pun) fish out of water.

Size and Longevity

Koi can grow quite large and live an astonishing amount of time if given proper care and living conditions. On average, they reach 24-

Note the tri-colored appearance of this sanke koi.

36 inches in length and live around 35-45 years, but some venerable old specimens achieve 4 feet in length and live well over 100 years. One exceptionally long-lived koi, named Hanako, is claimed to have been around for more than 200 years! In case you're wondering, a fish's age can be determined by counting the growth rings on its scales–much the same way one might count the annual rings on a tree stump. However, a microscope is required to count the rings on a fish's scale.

Adaptability

Though you might suspect that such beautiful fish would be delicate and hard to maintain for the average pond keeper, koi are, in actuality, remarkably hardy fish. They will even survive over winter beneath the ice in northern climates, provided the pond doesn't freeze solid and a hole is made in the ice to allow gas exchange.

What koi cannot tolerate are rapid fluctuations in water parameters or quality. They're also very sensitive to chlorine or chloramine used to treat municipal water supplies, so water must be treated with a chemical dechlorinator before it is added to their pond.

Part 2

Caution must also be taken when applying lawn and garden chemicals, including fertilizers, pesticides, and herbicides, in the vicinity of the pond to ensure that they are not carried into the water by wind or rain. Whole schools of prized koi can be lost due to careless lawn and garden chemical application.

Appropriate Pond Size

Koi require a fairly substantial amount of water in order to thrive. At the very least, you should provide 100 gallons of well-oxygenated pond water for each koi; 200 gallons per fish is even better. The truly massive, long-lived show specimens of Japan are afforded as much as 400-gallons per fish! Keep in mind the rather considerable adult size of koi when you are planning your pond, and you won't likely end up with overstocking problems further down the road.

Pond depth is also an important consideration. A maximum water depth of 4 to 5 feet is desirable. Why so deep? For one thing, deeper water provides more consistent temperatures. For another, it gives koi a refuge from wading birds, raccoons, and other creatures that might want to make a meal out of them.

Conducting proper research before you dig will assist you in choosing the right sized pond.

Part 2

Filtration and Water Changes

Substantial mechanical and biological filtration is needed to keep the water in a koi pond crystal clear. After all, koi can be a costly investment, and you don't want the beautiful colors of your fish to be lost in the murk. Even more important, water that isn't properly filtered can soon become toxic to the koi, especially if they are fed too frequently and/or too heavily.

The purpose of the mechanical filter is to remove suspended debris from the pond that would otherwise foul the water and harbor organisms that might be hazardous to the health of koi.

Biological filtration is also necessary, as discussed in previous chapters. To recap, biological filtration depends on the nitrogen cycle, which begins when toxic ammonia produced by fish urine and feces, rotting food, and other decomposing organic material is converted by a type of aerobic bacteria to a slightly less toxic compound called nitrite. Then, another type of aerobic bacteria converts the nitrite to an even less toxic compound called nitrate, which is then diluted through water changes and used by water plants for fertilizer.

In order for this process to work, the beneficial nitrifying bacteria must have a suitable substrate and, being aerobic, plenty of oxygenated water. These conditions are created within the biological filter, which passes a steady flow of oxygenated water over a porous medium that provides ample surface area for nitrifying bacteria to colonize.

As I just mentioned, water changes are required to dilute nitrate. So how much water should you change, and how often should you change it? Most koi pond experts recommend changing 10 to 25 percent of your pond's volume every week. Also, it's better to make smaller, more frequent water changes rather than larger, less frequent changes. Remember, stability of water parameters is desired in the koi pond, and larger water changes mean more stress on the koi due to greater swings in temperature, pH, and so on.

Pondmates for Koi

Koi will cohabit peacefully with goldfish and non-aggressive tropical fish that are too large to be swallowed easily. One wonders, though, whether any less dramatically colored goldfish or tropicals wouldn't suffer by comparison.

If you plan to add goldfish to the koi pond, choose varieties that have sleek, streamlined bodies, such as the comets and fantails, rather than varieties with bubble eyes or unnaturally rounded bodies, such as the orandas and lionheads, which don't tend to fare well in the pond setting.

The shubunkin is a calico-colored form of the common goldfish and does quite well in ponds with koi.

Part 2

Feeding koi should be fun and enjoyable for the whole family.

Feeding Koi

Koi quickly learn to associate the arrival of food with the person who brings the food–i.e., the pond keeper–and seem to be perpetually hungry, gaping their mouths at the surface and begging in an almost puppy-like fashion. Who could resist rewarding such endearing behavior as often and abundantly as possible? The pond keeper who wants to keep his koi alive and healthy, that's who! One of the most common mistakes made by koi keepers, and aquarists in general, is "loving their scaly charges to death" by overfeeding.

Koi should be fed a staple diet of floating pellets specifically formulated to meet their dietary needs. Some koi keepers also supplement dry food with peas, spinach, and other vegetable foods. Feed no more than the fish can consume within approximately five minutes. Also, it's preferable to offer two or three light feedings each day rather than one heavy feeding. If you feed too heavily, some of the pellets will get waterlogged, sink to the bottom and decompose to the detriment of water quality.

Overwintering

It may seem like harsh treatment for such stunning fish, but koi are perfectly capable of surviving in the pond over winter in cold climes, provided a few simple steps are taken to get them ready for Jack Frost's debut.

Koi enter a state of semi-hibernation in winter, and their diet must be adjusted with the dropping temperature. Once temperatures fall below 50°F in autumn, stop feeding high-protein foods, which will remain undigested in the fishes' bellies if offered too late in the season. Instead, offer wheat germ to your koi until winter sets in. Then, cut off your feedings altogether until the following spring. The koi will meet their meager nutritional needs in winter by nibbling on natural items in the pond.

What about the inevitable freezing of the pond? Your koi will do just fine if the surface of the pond freezes as long as the entire pond doesn't freeze solid. Also, be sure to create a hole in the ice to allow oxygen to enter the water and noxious gasses to escape. It's very important to make the hole by pouring warm water onto one spot on the ice rather than by breaking a hole in the surface. Breaking the ice will send a shockwave through the pond that can injure or even kill your koi.

The Japanese are world leaders in koi breeding as evidence by ponds such as this.

Part 2

How to Beat the High Cost of Koi

What do you do if you're fascinated by the multi-colored spectacle of a well-stocked koi pond but you simply don't have the funds to purchase more than a few good-quality fish? Well, unless you plan to breed show-quality koi, there's absolutely nothing wrong with starting out with specimens that have a somewhat less-prestigious lineage. Most of the koi stocked and sold at your local water garden center will fall into this category. Sure, they may not hold up to the purist's scrutiny, but they can be quite charming in their own right, and, besides, you'll still have some money left over for fish food after you buy them.

Part Three

Your Pond in Nature

by Michael S. Paletta

"I know this garden pond is great and all, but it would be a lot better with a changing station."

A Pond For All Seasons

A carefully planned and designed pond is much more than a container for water–it is a water garden that should be an integral part of an overall landscape plan. As with any well thought-out garden plan, it should be visually appealing all year round. Even when the pond is "shut down" for winter, the area around it can

Your pond should be able to remain cool in summer, but as warm as possible in winter.

Ponds should be exposed to at least a few hours of direct sunlight each day.

still provide enjoyable viewing and be the focal point of any landscape.

In order to maximize the pleasure of viewing a pond, all types of plants should be utilized. These include not only the water plants, but also trees, shrubs, and perennials or annuals that will make the landscape around the pond complete. There are several goals for planting around or in a pond, stream, or waterfall. One goal is to have the planting make the pond look like a natural part of the landscape rather than being a manmade addition. They should also aid in making the water portion look like part of the landscape that has always been there. Another goal of planting should be for the plants to help filter the water and provide food or shelter and a natural habitat for the fish. Lastly, the plants should help to provide an attraction for wildlife to the pond and should do this without adding unnecessary work for the pond keeper.

Trees

The first groups of plants that need to be taken into account when planning the landscape around a pond are the trees. Seeing dappled sunlight pass through the trees and onto the water can provide the feeling that you are deep in a forest and not just in your backyard.

Having a few trees near the pond can also provide much needed shade for the pond during the hot summer. When a pond, waterfall, or stream is incorporated properly along a strand of older trees, it can look like it has always been there. Even having a single tree near a pond can dramatically increase the amount of wildlife that visits the pond, so there should always be some trees nearby. Having evergreens near a pond can also help to provide winter color and a focal point when all of the other trees have lost their leaves and all of the perennials and pond plants are dormant.

Unfortunately, there are also some negatives to having trees near a pond. First and foremost among these is the dirt and leaves that will find their way into the pond. These become especially troublesome as the trees become larger and produce greater and greater quantities of leaves each fall. In addition some trees, such as oak, produce leaves that can dramatically affect the water quality should a large quantity of them reach the pond. The needles from evergreens have a similar effect. Some trees also produce very invasive roots that can damage the pond's foundation. Therefore, when considering the planting of trees near a pond these negatives need to taken into account and planned for accordingly.

In order to minimize these problems, the pond should be far enough away from the trees so that the majority of leaves from the trees do not fall directly into the pond and their thicker roots stay far enough away from the foundation to minimize any possible damage. The size to which the trees will grow should be taken into

Part 3

Ponds with overhanging branches will have a buildup of leaves during autumn.

account when the planting is done to minimize the amount of leaves falling directly into the pond. Screening can be placed over the pond for the two weeks in autumn when most of the leaves drop so that they can be kept from accumulating in the pond. As with everything in a pond, when planning is done properly, the desired goal can be achieved.

Bushes and Shrubs

Like trees, bushes or shrubs play a role in making a pond look natural. These plants can provide small areas of shade; can be placed so that some of their branches overhang the pond, and they can be used to hide large pieces of equipment like filter boxes or sterilizers. In addition, they offer an advantage over trees in that if they get too large or become invasive, they are much easier to remove or replace.

There are many small evergreens, including hollies, pines, and boxwoods, that provide foliage around a pond even in winter. In addition, there are some bushes, such as the red or green twigged dogwoods, that also provide an interesting contrast in winter, due to the vivid coloration of their branches. There are also numerous bushes that are good for providing winter interest due to the color or texture of their bark that is only visible after their leaves have

Part 3

dropped. Lastly, several bushes such as Clethra and Weigela can also add not only beautiful flowers but also wonderful fragrances that add to the total experience of the pond. These plants will also add to the dirt in the pond when they drop their leaves in the fall, but the amount they produce is significantly less than those of the trees. For these reasons, a few shrubs should always be utilized when landscaping a pond.

Bushes and shrubbery look great, but take care to keep these plants trimmed and healthy.

Perennials and Annuals

While trees and shrubs are part of the big picture of landscaping a pond, perennials and annuals are the plants that can really make a pond stand out when they are used properly. One interesting aspect of keeping a water garden is that it allows for keeping plants that can't be kept in a terrestrial garden.

However, the plants used to aquascape or landscape a pond are quite diverse and vary dramatically depending upon where the pond is located. Plants that are annuals in the north may be perennials in the south. Some plants that are fine to use in the north due to their dying out every winter are considered pests in the south and may even be illegal to keep there. Therefore, in order to under-

Part 3

Different flowers come into bloom at different times, so plant accordingly for maximum effect.

stand which plants should be used, it is necessary to classify them. Plants for the pond can be separated by three criteria: hardiness, light requirements, and water requirements.

Hardiness actually refers to cold hardiness, which is how cold can the temperature be and have the plant survive. If you look in any plant catalog, you will see a zone map designed by the U.S. Department of Agriculture. It lays out a grid of 11 zones, each specifying the average coldest temperature that a zone will experience each winter. Zone 11 has the highest average winter temperature and Zone 1 has the coldest. For example, in Zone 6, the average winter temperature is 0 to 10°F. When choosing plants that are considered to be perennials, the zone for which they are chosen should at least match the zone you are in. That is if you are in Zone 6, you should choose plants that are hardy enough to survive in Zone 6 or lower zones, such as 5. It should be noted that many factors could cause these zones to vary by as many as two. These factors include altitude, wind exposure, snow cover, soil types, etc. So even though a plant might be considered hardy for a specific zone, an exceptionally cold winter with little snow cover can dramatically reduce its hardiness.

Part 3

Just as temperature can affect a plant's hardiness, so can its exposure to light. Most plants require at least some sunlight, and this light requirement can be further categorized into whether they require full sun, part shade, or full shade. Plants that require full sun require at least six hours of direct sunlight per day in the south and eight hours in the north to grow and bloom their best. Plants requiring partial shade need two to four hours of sunlight or dappled shade. Full-shade plants do not tolerate more than an hour or so of sunlight and do best when they receive indirect light. Like the temperature hardiness, the light requirements will be present on the tags of the plant when it is purchased.

Rooted Emergent Plants

Rooted emergent plants are plants that are commonly rooted in large pots or other suitable planting containers. These containers should not be placed too deep or the tubers may not take properly. The main difference between these and floating emergent plants is that rooted emergent plants are always connected by long stems to their bulbs, while "floaters" just float freely around the pond controlled only by water currents and wind. During winter months, tropical species must be brought indoors or they will die off completely. Hardy lilies on the other hand, are normally quite tolerant of cold temperatures down to and even well below the freezing mark.

Water Lilies

The most popular pond plant and the one that attracts the most people to the hobby is the water lily. The beauty of their flowers along with the lily pads for frogs to sit on make them the most desirable plant for just about every pond. These plants come in a wide variety of sizes and produce flowers with just about every color in the rainbow. The variance in size can be quite dramatic with sizes ranging from dwarf (2 to 3-inch leaves) to large (8 to 10-inch leaves). Care should be taken to make sure that the plant's size matches that of the pond in which it will be kept.

Lilies have flowers that bloom during the day, flowers that bloom at night, and even some flowers with amazing scents. The day bloomers have flowers that open soon after sunrise and close right before sunset. They can be grown by either planting their roots or tuber in the substrate at the bottom of a pond or by placing the tuber in a pot. Planting is quite simple in that all that is really required is to place the tuber in good-quality garden soil or specially made pond soil so that the substrate covers most of the tuber but allows for the leave to emerge. Once they start to develop a good set of roots and leaves and flowers emerge, special water lily fertilizer tablets should be added to their substrate regularly to allow for maximum growth.

Red-flowered lilies represent some of the most popular variants.

Lilies come in both winter hardy and tropical varieties, and once they start growing they can reproduce quite rapidly. The best way to tell the difference in unmarked varieties is that winter hardy varieties usually have smooth, rounded leaves, while tropical varieties have notched or pointed tips to their leaves. It is usually best to start off with the native or winter hardy varieties, as these are the least demanding and will easily winter over in

Healthy lilies will easily spread over the water's surface.

the pond. These plants usually do best in full, strong sun, but some will tolerate a bit of shade. All that is necessary is that once a hard frost kills off the foliage and the flowers, this dead material is removed and the pot should be lowered to the bottom of the pond for winter. If the lily is planted in the substrate, then all that is necessary is to remove the dead leaves once they have been killed by a frost.

Once the water warms up in the spring, potted lilies should be moved up from the bottom of the pond to where they will get stronger light. Soon, shoots will emerge from the tuber, and soon thereafter, leaves will start to form at the surface. At this time, the tubers can be separated into several smaller tubers to produce more

Part 3

lilies. All that is necessary is a sharp knife to cut the tubers into equal-sized sections, each of which should contain budding leaves. In late May or early June, when the water has warmed significantly, flowers will start to bloom. At this point, they can be moved back to deeper levels to allow for other plants to be placed in the shallows, or they can be left alone.

It should be noted that while lilies are often kept with koi, most koi find the stems and leaves quite tasty and will frequently eat the leaves and stems to such a degree that the lilies never reach their full potential. Even the flowers themselves will be eaten by many koi. To keep this from being a problem, it may be necessary to set up some type of barrier to prevent the koi from decimating the lilies. As an alternative, the lilies can be allowed to grow in an area separate from the koi until they have grown out enough larger, tougher leaves that will typically be less palatable to the koi before the plants are placed with them.

Also water lilies prefer to grow in calm water, so they should not be placed where there is strong current from streams or waterfalls. When these conditions are met, water lilies provide beautiful flowers and will do well for years with minimal care. In addition, their abundance of leaves on the surface help to provide shade and keep the pond cool. This shade also produces another beneficial effect in that it reduces the amount of sun hitting the substrate, so this helps to keep algae levels down as well. If alga blooms becomes problematic, one of the ways to reduce it is to have the surface

Part 3

covered with a lot of lilies. This, along with the lilies removing nutrients from the water, can help to rapidly get algae under control.

Water Lotus

A plant that is a special species of water lily is the water lotus. Looking similar to other water lilies initially, over the growing season, this plant becomes much more spectacular. This large plant produces leaves that stand high above the water. More impressive is that in midsummer it produces fragrant blossoms that can reach up to 12 inches across. Up until recently, this plant was not kept in many ponds, especially those with soil bottoms, as its root growth could be quite invasive (in some soil ponds it could spread over 30 feet in a single growing season). Now, however, it is grown in containers, which keeps its invasive nature in check.

In order to grow these impressive plants, the lotus roots should be placed in a 10-gallon planting pot filled with heavy clay loam soil. Above this, a light layer of gravel should be placed to keep the clay from being washed away. After planting the lotus, it should be placed in water that is not less than 4 inches or more than 10 inches deep. Once the lotus is established and the leaves have reached the surface, it can be placed in its final position 12 to 18 inches below the surface of the water. The ultimate size of the lotus will be determined not only by the variety of the plant, but also by the water depth, soil volume, pruning, and the frequency with which fertilizer is applied, so the gardener can actually help determine how large the lotus grows.

Part 3

Water lotus, a very popular species of emergent plant, reaches sizable proportions.

This perennial is winter hardy to at least Zone 6 if it is submerged under enough water all winter. In addition to its beautiful fragrant flowers, once the flowers fade after their six to eight weeks of blooming, their exotic seed head remains. Lotuses come in a wide range of colors including white, blue, pink, and red. So for anyone with a large pond that is looking for a dramatic centerpiece plant, the water lotus is an ideal choice.

Floating Hearts

A smaller, winter-hardy cousin of the water lily is the floating heart (*Nymphoides peltata*). These plants require the same basic care as the water lilies, but they grow much smaller. For this reason, they are great, submerged plants to use for decorating the middle of smaller ponds. Not only do their leaves not get too big, but the tubers remain relatively small as well, so the pots they are planted in do not need to be too large either. These plants produce small white or yellow flowers throughout the growing season. They are widely available and should be used anywhere that space is at a premium.

Floating Emergent Plants

While lilies can be used exclusively to cover the surface of a pond, there are also a wide variety of other plants that can be considered that simply float in the water. These plants do not require any pots or soil in which to grow and are desirable not only for this, but also because they are relatively easy to grow. These plants are not only attractive, but they also help to reduce algae by rapidly consuming nutrients. In fact, many of these plants can be used as a biofilter.

In order to do this all that is necessary is to place these plants in an area where the fish will not eat them and where water from the pond will flow past them. As the water flows past these plants, remove the nitrogen and phosphate that is produced in the waste material from the fish. Because they are more efficient at consuming this waste than are the lower plants, they basically starve out the algae and keep it from becoming a problem.

There are, however, some shortcomings of using these plants. First, they can grow quite rapidly, and if they are not controlled, they can overwhelm a pond. In a closed pond this is usually not a problem because the excess plants simply need to be removed on a regular basis. In open ponds and especially in the south, this can be a problem in that if these get into wild waterways, they can completely overtake a body of water. Another potential problem is that many of these plants are not cold tolerant, and if they are not removed before the first hard frost, they can rapidly die.

Because they can grow to very large numbers if they are not removed before this, their death and rapid decay can easily foul a pond and kill the fish. Conversely, when these plants are first added

Part 3

On the average, water hyacinth grows to approximately the diameter of a dinner plate.

to a pond the koi can eat them all before they become established, so as mentioned above, they should be started in a partitioned-off area until they become established. Once they are growing profusely, they can be thinned and thrown in for the koi to eat.

Water Hyacinth

One of the most rapid growing and most popular of the floating plants is the water hyacinth. This lovely plant has bright-green foliage that looks like it has a thin coat of wax on it, along with large, lavender flowers that stand up above the foliage. These flowers are produced throughout the summer. This plant stops growing once the temperature falls and dies as soon as there is a light frost. It is not easy to keep it alive indoors during the winter, so it should be considered an annual anywhere below Zone 8. These plants are one of the best plants for the above-described biofilter in that they possess long fibrous roots that take up a lot of nutrients. For this and because of their beautiful flowers, they are a great choice for just about every pond.

Water Lettuce

Another plant that is great for use in the biofilter and that is only slightly less attractive than the water hyacinth is water lettuce

Part 3

(*Pistia stratiotes*). This plant, like its name implies, looks nothing more than a large head of floating lettuce. The beauty of this plant, at least in the north, is that it is such a vigorous grower with such vigorous roots that it can remove so much of the pond's excess nutrients, which, unless kept in a pond with an abundance of fish, may need to be removed

Water lettuce is intolerant of cool temperatures.

from time to be fertilized. This is indicated if the plants start to fade from its customary bright green coloration to a pale yellow. If this occurs, the plants should be removed from the pond and placed in a separate container where liquid fertilizer is added until the plants return to their vivid, green hue.

In the fall after the first frost, these plants will die off quickly, so as with the hyacinths they need to be rapidly removed from the pond before they decay and foul the pond. These plants cannot be kept in the south, as they are so invasive that if they get loose into a natural waterway, they can seriously damage these ecosystems. These plants also do not winter well indoors, so it is usually best to simply purchase one or two of these plants every spring and allow them to reproduce on their own.

Part 3

Fairy Moss

Another excellent plant for keeping algae in check is fairy moss (*Azolla caroliniana*). Unlike the other two, this plant does not keep algae in check by removing large of waste, but rather it rapidly grows over the entire surface of a pond and keeps the algae in check by limiting the amount of sunlight that penetrates. It acts to fill in areas between other plants and grows just about anywhere there is sunlight and space. Unlike the other two plants, fairy moss is winter hardy to Zone 5, but it will still die back in this zone if there is not adequate snow cover or if there is strong wind, which will cause the exposed surface to dry out and burn. Therefore, it may be a good idea to remove a significant portion of these plants before winter to keep the die off to a minimum.

Other Popular Floating Plants

Some other floating plants include Frog's bit (*Limnobium spongia*), Butterfly Fern (*Salvinia rotundifolia*), Duckweed (*Lemna minor*), Rosette Water Lettuce (*Pistia* spp.) and Anacharis (*Elodea* spp.). These plants share many of the characteristics of the above listed floaters in that they grow rapidly and help to reduce algae growth. Most of these should be considered annuals in the north, so they should be removed from the pond soon after the first frost.

Marginal Plants

The last and possibly most interesting groups of plants for decorating a pond are the marginal or bog plants. More precisely, these should be called the emergent plants, because their roots are underwater or in wet areas, while the main body of the plant emerges from the water. These plants can be grown in areas where the water is shallow, such as on the edges of the pond or even just in areas that get extra moisture, such as where the pond overflows after a rainstorm. These plants are quite useful for landscaping a pond due to their versatility and wide variety of looks, and

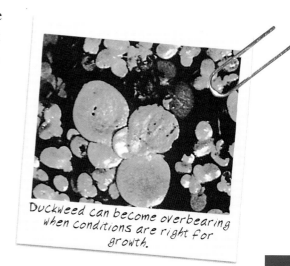

Duckweed can become overbearing when conditions are right for growth.

they can help to soften the line of where land and water meet. They can be grown as single specimens, or they can be grown massed in borders where their number can be quite dramatic. Marginals can also be used to provide an interesting backdrop for small ponds.

They come in a wide variety of sizes and shapes and can be anything from the exotic black elephant ear (*Colocasia esculenta*) to the common Cattail (*Typha latifolia*). They can be shade-loving carnivorous plants like the pitcher plant (*Sarracenia* spp.) and Venus flytrap (*Dionae muscipula*) to the sun-loving Pickeral Rush (*Pontederia cordata*). The only thing that these plants have in common is that their roots must remain moist for them to thrive. Many of the most beautiful are tropical in origin, which is not surprising, because when you think of swamps you typically think of warm, tropical areas. Many of the tropical varieties can be over-wintered indoors, and many of the shade-loving tropical, bog plants have been kept for years as houseplants. Fortunately, many of these once-rare plants are now readily available, as there are now nurseries devoted to growing plants exclusively for the pond hobby, so they no longer need to be taken from the wild. Fortunately, they are easy to grow and produce, so their price has come down dramatically in recent years.

Ponds can be incor-porated into sloping landscapes as well.

The other fortunate aspect about these plants is that once they are established, they require little care. All should be grown in pots because if they are placed on an earth bottom, they can become invasive. Initially, once they are planted in a pot, they should be placed at minimal water depth, with the surface water not being more than 1 to 2 inches above their surface. Once they are established, they can be lowered to their maximum water depth, which is usually not more than 10 to 12 inches. They should be fertilized not more than once per month. However, it should be noted that due to their rapid growth and strong ability to remove nutrients, such as phosphorus and nitrogen, many pond keepers are now also using these plants to build bog filters.

Bog Filters

It has been known for a long time that bogs can be polluted with dirty water and that over time the plants in these bogs render the water pure. Therefore, in an effort to get the same effect in ponds full of fish and to reduce the amount of work required, some pond enthusiasts set up part of their pond to act as a bog filter. This may sound like a lot of work, but in reality it is quite simple and ingenious. All that is really required is for a section of the pond to be shallow with some flow across it, and in this shallow area, a heavy planting of known, heavy-feeding bog plants are planted. Over time, the plants in this bog grow, and as they do, they remove waste and pollutants from the water. This filter not only helps to remove waste and thus lessen the need for water changes, but it also

Gunnera manicata is a species often used in bog filters with great success.

Part 3

Be sure to not have too many plants in your bog filter.

produces luxuriant plants that make something that is usually not appealing to look at, a filter, something that can be quite spectacular. This shallow area should be filled with gravel, as this helps in the establishment of bacteria that convert waste material into forms that the plants can readily utilize.

In order to maximize the efficiency of this bog filter, it should have between 10 to 20 percent of the surface area of the main pond and not more than 12 inches deep. The plants should be taken out of their pots and their root balls should be placed directly in the gravel. A combination of tall plants with fibrous roots and short, fast-growing plants should be used to maximize nutrient uptake. Some good plants that have been found to work the best in these types of filters are Lemon Bacopa (*Bacopa caroliniana*), Purple Iris (*Iris veriscolor*) Chameleon plant (*Houttuynia cordata*), and *Lysmachia nummilaria*. Most of these plants are not only useful at removing nutrients, but they are quite attractive as well. A properly done bog filter is not only attractive, but it can also help to transition the pond into the neighboring terrestrial landscape.

Just about any emergent plant can be used in this type of filter, and

Part 3

there are large numbers of just about every type of plant to choose from. The most common and easy-to-keep marginal plants include these hardy varieties: Arrowhead (*Sagittaria* spp.), Pickeral Rush (*Pontederia cordata*), Horsetail Rush (*Equisetum hyemale*), Water Mint (*Mentha aquatica*), Water celery (*Oenathea javanica*), Variegated Sweet flag (*Acorus variegates*), and any of the water Iris species. Some good tropical marginals are: Ruby creeper (*Alternathera rubra*), the Taros (*Colocasia* spp.), Umbrella palm (*Cyperus alternifolius*), Water zinnia (*Wedelia trilobata*), and any of the Cannas (*Canna* sp.). Some of the tropical marginals that will even do well in shade include Black Magic Taro (*Colocasia esculenta*), Sensitive Plant (*Neptunia aquatica*), and Aquatic Morning Glory (*Ipomea batatas*).

With this wide of a variety of plants that live in the shallow area of a pond, it is possible to find a suitable plant for just about any area of the pond. While these plants do best with their roots submerged, there is also a wide variety of plants that simply like their roots to be constantly moist. These plants will do their best at the very edges of the pond and

Cattails, *Typha angustifolia*, are another common and hardy marginal plant species.

will further help to soften the edges of the pond. While not thought of as pond plants, they can nonetheless help in the total landscaping of the pond. These plants include the astilbes, day lilies, *Hostas*, buddleias, and the loosestrifes. It should be noted that purple loosestrife could become very invasive if grown in the moist area around a pond. However, it can be controlled if it is containerized. A better choice for growth in the moist area surrounding a pond is Gooseneck loosestrife.

Planting Suggestions

When trying to plant and landscape around a pond, it is necessary to understand that it will take time for the plants to grow in and for the pond to become fully integrated into the landscape. For this reason, care should be taken to not add too many plants initially, because in the optimum conditions of most ponds, the plants will grow rapidly. If too many plants are chosen or planted, the result will be a mismatched hodgepodge of plants.

Planters with medium-sized edging plants are often used to cover water tubing or electrical cords.

Initially in the first year, a small group of not more than four or five different plants should be chosen and planted and allowed to grow both in and around the pond. Once these are established, one or two more can be added in subsequent years until the landscaping is complete. If, over time, any of the plants become too invasive or are unattractive, they simply can be removed. This is done much more easily if only a few plants are present than if a large number is present. This is why it is so useful to go slow.

Ponds in the open will require an assortment of plants to help regulate light and temperature.

One other aspect of planting a pond to be enjoyed year round that should not be overlooked is to view as many ponds and streams as possible before beginning to plant your own. This will give you an idea of what certain plants look like as they mature and also how plants do in your area. By viewing both manmade and natural ponds and streams, you can also get an idea of how to integrate your own pond or stream into your landscape. This requires a little extra effort initially, but it will pay off in the long run. Planting a pond is only slightly different than planting other landscape, but the sense of accomplishment one feels the first time a water lily or lotus blooms is more rewarding than just about any other type of gardening and well worth the extra effort.

Excellent Aquariums

start with

with

TROPICAL FISH

HOBBYIST

SAVE UP TO
63%

BUSINESS REPLY MAIL
FIRST-CLASS MAIL   PERMIT NO. 65   NEPTUNE, NJ

TROPICAL FISH HOBBYIST
SUBSCRIPTION DIVISION
P.O. Box 427
Neptune, NJ 07754-9989

A Walk on the Wild Side

One of the essential goals of setting up a pond or other water-based system is to have it look as natural as possible. To achieve this, plants of many different types are cultivated in and around the water and all mechanical equipment, such as filters or plumbing, are hidden from view. Over time, the pond becomes more and more

Raccoons are often tough to deter, so sometimes it's better to accommodate them.

naturalized so that eventually it looks like it has always been part of the natural landscape. The main reason why some ponds still do not look natural is because, despite all of the effort, it lacks having wildlife around it.

Fortunately, as greater experience has been garnered in the keeping of ponds, a better understanding of how to attract wildlife has been achieved. Different types of wildlife require different elements to be in place in order to be attracted to a pond. A well-developed pond and accompanying landscape will attract not only birds and mammals, but also amphibians, reptiles, and insects. While these latter three groups of animals may not at first seem appealing, it is only when the entire ecosystem is present that a pond will look natural.

Attracting Wildlife to Your Pond

All animals require three basic things: food, water, and shelter. When establishing a pond in a landscape and planting it properly, usually all three of these must be present. However, despite our best intentions, only some ponds attract a wide variety of animals and birds, while others seem devoid of these creatures. The answer may be in how the pond area is planted and how the pond is designed. In order for the larger animals to be present, the food chain has to be present from the bottom up.

Insects

It is necessary for many species of insects to be present to help start the food chain (it should be noted that insects themselves are not the foundation of a food chain; however, they are the smallest, visible symbols of a healthy beginning). The reason why some ponds attract insects and others do not seems to be a function of how many native plants are present. That is, if a pond is full of plants that are not native to that area, these plants seem to act as a natural insecticide and keep the population of insects down. Some people will think it is good that their pond is not attracting insects, especially mosquitoes, but in reality, if there are no insects, there will also be fewer amphibians like frogs and salamanders and also birds and bats, all of which eat insects. When there are fewer of these animals present, there will also be fewer of the higher animals present that eat them.

Planting with Native Plants

The first step for establishing a habitat for wildlife is to plant it with native plants. Fortunately, there are lots of interesting native plants that can be used in and around ponds to attract insects and other wildlife. These include native herbaceous plants for sunny locations like Cattails *(Typhus* spp.), Joe-Pye weed *(Eupatorium maculatum)*, Cardinal flower *(Lobelia cardinalis)*, Goldenrods (Solidago spp.), and Marsh Marigolds *(Caltha palustris)*. There are also similar plants for shady locations including: Bee balm *(Monarda didyma)*, Turtlehead *(Chelone* spp.), Royal fern *(Osmunda regalis)*, Jack-in-the-pulpit *(Arisaema triphyllum)*, and False hellebore *(Veratrum viride)*. It is not necessary to have the landscape filled exclusively with native plants, but the higher the percentage of natives, the greater the likelihood of getting a full population of insects.

Fortunately, because most ponds contain fish and moving water to some degree, the establishment of a healthy pond usually diminishes the mosquito population. This happens for two reasons. First, if the mosquitoes lay their eggs in the pond, when the larvae hatch, the fish will eat them because their larvae are one of their favorite foods. Second, if the pond is set up properly, it will attract amphibians and birds. Both of these consume large quantities of adult mosquitoes. As a result, once a pond is established, the mosquito population around it will actually be less than a similar area without a healthy pond.

Part 3

Insects serve a very important role in a pond's overall health.

Some of the interesting insects that may be attracted to a pond and its properly landscaped surroundings include dragonflies, damselflies, butterflies, beetles, moths, bees and wasps. While these last four insects may not all be considered pond-owner friendly, they are vital to the overall ecosystem. Of these, the most interesting are the dragonflies and damselflies. With their translucent wings that reflect light like a prism, they are everyone's favorite pond insects. The only thing necessary to attract them to a pond is to provide some floating plants or leaves within the water so that they have a place to attach their eggs. Even if a pond is relatively far from a natural water source, they somehow seem to find their way to every pond. Having them present is usually an indicator that the quality of the water in the pond is good.

Amphibians

Similarly, when conditions are good, amphibians, such as frogs and toads, will appear. They, like the dragonfly, are drawn to water from great distances. In the case of frogs, it is probably due to the sound of running water. Each spring, bullfrogs and spring peepers migrate, and if your pond is up and running early enough to catch this migration, you may be blessed (though some might say cursed) with the twilight calls of these frogs. In an attempt to lure a female, the small males will let out a chorus that is unmistakable.

Bullfrogs can be rather pugnacious pond residents.

Amphibians need shallow, well-planted areas in which to lay their eggs and hide, as well as cool moist areas in which to hunt insects. These animals are currently dropping in numbers worldwide due to the destruction of their habitat. In order to help them recover, restoration of their habitat is essential. Even if this habitat is only partially restored in a backyard pond, it will help bring back the frogs.

Frogs are also on the menu for a wide variety of animals and birds. To further increase the likelihood of their survival, some cover should be present for them as well. This can be in the form of dense vegetation along the edge of a pond or rockwork along the edge, which provides them with small caves where they can hide. In addition, these animals like to burrow in the mud in the shallows of the pond during the winter. If frogs are present in your pond throughout the summer, a shallow tray of mud should be placed in the shallows in the fall so that they have a place to hibernate.

Part 3

Ducks, geese, and swans can really disrupt a pond's water chemistry.

Birds

While insects and amphibians can be induced to visit even a small pond when the proper conditions are provided, it takes more in terms of landscaping and preparation in order to attract desirable birds and mammals to a pond. As noted above, all animals require food, water, and shelter in order to survive. Therefore, in order to attract wildlife to your pond, it may be necessary to do a little more in order to attract these higher animals.

Ponds are a natural attractant to many birds if a few conditions are provided. First, birds are attracted to moving water rather than stagnant pools. This seems to be a function of the sound of moving water rather than the actual motion itself, so some means should be provided to produce the sound of moving water. This can be as simple as having a small pump that causes the water to splash or as elaborate as having a large pump that produces a waterfall. This sound will initially attract the birds, and then in order to keep them, the pond needs to be bird friendly. A pond should have a shallow area not more than an inch deep where the birds can wade in to bathe. This area should also have a rough surface so that when they do so, they can feel secure and not slip into the water. The pond should also be free of algae as well, and the area should also be in

Part 3

the open away from any plants. This allows the birds to feel secure and also keeps any neighborhood cats from getting an easy meal.

Plants and Fruit

In addition to providing water, a source for food for the birds is also essential for attracting them. Birds eat a wide variety of fruits and seeds, as well as insects, so several different types of plants should be provided to feed them throughout the season. Hawthorns, dogwoods, and elderberries are three good plants for this purpose. The seeds most birds prefer are not suitable for planting, as they are more agricultural than aesthetic, such as millet or corn. However, some plants, such as sunflowers and angelicas, produce seeds on plants that can actually be quite attractive. A wide selection of fruit-bearing plants for birds should be chosen with a wide variety of ripening times for the berries and fruit. Some berries should ripen in the summer, while others should have fruits that persist into the fall and winter.

Blackberries, mulberries, and other similar berries are generally rich in high-energy sugars, are relished by many forms of wildlife, and ripen in the early to mid-summer. Because of their high sugar content they rot quickly if they are not consumed. Typical fall and winter fruits include hollies, hawthorns, and viburnums that have fruits generally composed of low-energy lipids, which resist rot. The fruits from these plants persist well into the cold weather and are eaten by birds and mammals when nothing else is available in the winter. By spring, these fruits have often dried out and look

Ducks regularly feed on aquatic vegetation, as this duck is demonstrating here.

shriveled, but because there is even less to eat in the late spring, they may still be consumed.

There are only a few plants that have fall-ripening fruits containing high-energy lipids that would rot if not eaten. These include dogwood, sassafras, Virginia creeper, and black gum. The hypothesis for why these plants contain these high-energy fruits in the fall is also why they may turn colors earlier than the other plants. By doing so, they draw attention to themselves and attract migratory birds (that need lots of energy for migration), and so by attracting these birds and having them eat their fruit, they get the best dispersal of their seed possible. Therefore by planting these plants with fall–ripening fruit, it is possible to attract birds that might otherwise not be seen regularly in your area.

In addition to attracting migratory birds it is also possible to attract everyone's favorite bird, the hummingbird, to a properly designed landscape. These birds require lots of food, but unlike other birds, they feed almost exclusively on nectar. To reach the nectar in many flowers, they have a specially designed beak that allows them to reach into the deep innermost areas of a flower. As a result, they can reach the nectar that eludes most other birds.

Hummingbirds

In order to attract hummingbirds, a wide variety of plants that produce tubular flowers should be planted. These flowers should be pink, orange, yellow, or red in color, as these are the colors most attractive to hummingbirds. Some plants that meet these criteria include Columbine, Salvia, Bee balm, Digitalis, Lobelia Lilies, and Honeysuckle. Nectar is not exclusively eaten by hummingbirds, however, as over 60 species of birds have also been found to feed on nectar. Therefore, in order to attract other nectar feeding birds, plants that produce an abundance of flowers full of nectar should also be planted. These include Weigala, Clethra, Daphne, Trumpet vine, and Bellflowers. Plantings of several different types of these plants should be done so that as bloom of one type of flower ends, another takes its place. By doing this, the stay of the hummingbirds and other nectar-feeding birds can be prolonged, in addition to having different flowers in bloom all summer long.

Providing Cover and Shelter

While having plants provide food is essential for attracting birds, so is providing cover. Most birds do not like being out in the open, as it makes them an easy target for predators, such as hawks, falcons, and owls. Birds also need cover in order to reproduce. For a pond landscape to be complete in terms of attracting birds, it also has to provide adequate cover. Cover and shelter for birds does not simply mean trees or brush for them to hide in or reproduce. A proper landscape to attract birds needs to be layered. That is, a landscape that induces birds to stay needs to be more that just tall trees and grass. Birds require shrubs, bushes, and plants to fill in much of the space between the ground and the trees in order for them to feel comfortable.

Not all birds nest in the highest trees, so the trees also need to be of different heights. The tree selection should contain both deciduous and evergreen trees to allow for some cover during the winter and also to provide points of interest. If no evergreens are present, the landscape looks especially stark during the long winter months. The massed plantings of shrubs should have different-sized branches, as this will allow birds of different sizes to perch on them. The key for attracting birds is to have the space around the trees full of plants but with space for the birds to fly.

As with other plants discussed earlier, native trees and shrubs should be the first choice. Fortunately, there are a wide variety of native trees and shrubs that are especially attractive for birds. These include American beech (*Fagus grandifolia*), Black gum (*Nyssa sylvatica*), Crabapple (*Malus* spp.), Flowering dogwoods (*Cornus florida*), Hawthorns (*Crataegus* spp.), Hickories (*Carya* spp.), Oaks (*Quercus* spp.), and Red Mulberry (*Morus rubra*). There are also several native shrubs that birds find attractive. These include Hollies (*Ilex* spp.), Junipers (*Juniperus* spp.), Spicebush (*Lindera benzoin*), Sumacs (*Rhus* spp.), Viburnums (*Viburnum* spp.), and Myrtles (*Myrica* spp.). The key with all of these is to plant groupings of shrubs or trees, not individuals. Groupings are not only more aesthetically pleasing, but they are also more likely to attract multiples of birds rather than individuals.

Nesting Sites

The last things necessary to attract birds are nesting sites. Setting these up, especially when establishing a landscape, can go a long way to induce birds to start to visit your landscape. Providing nesting areas and materials will also induce birds to visit and stay in your landscape. Once a bird begins nesting in a particular area, it will usually visit the

Providing a shelter for resident waterfowl is a good idea, especially if you want them to stay around.

same area each year, so if you can establish good nesting sites early, you can induce the same birds to visit year after year. Not all birds nest in the same sites or need the same nesting material, so before you get started, it is a good idea to determine which birds nest in your local area and what their requirements are.

Once this is done, you then need to set up birdhouses or nesting boxes in environments that are favored by the birds you want to attract. For example, bluebirds and red-winged blackbirds prefer nests in open fields with a few trees nearby on which they can perch. Chickadees and woodpeckers prefer to nest in brushy wooded areas. The nesting boxes should also have the holes leading into them of the appropriate size. If you want to get chickadees to nest, do not make the hole for their box large enough

Part 3

for a robin. The boxes should also be designed to be cat and squirrel-proof, as these animals will keep birds from nesting–or worse. Lastly, a wide variety of nesting material should be provided. This can include hay, hair, string, and bits of cloth or just about anything else small enough for the birds to haul and put in their nests. When all of these things are completed, the area around a pond will rapidly fill with birds and other animals.

Mammals

The other animals that may also be attracted to a landscaped pond area are small mammals. Chipmunks, squirrels, shrews, rabbits, foxes and the like will eventually find their way to the landscape around the pond if their needs are provided. Piles of rocks or logs will often act as nesting areas for these animals. Even a thick layer of mulch will often provide enough cover so that some of these animals settle in. These animals also like some open space to be present as well.

If a dead tree or stump is present or a log, these will also often be converted into homes by many animals. Because it may not be possible initially to have a dead tree present, it may be necessary to visit an area where new homes are being constructed and ask the builder if you may remove the dead trees or snags. Adding one or two of these to a landscape will add to the natural look of it, as well as providing a nesting area for many animals. Very few native animals live exclusively in the deep, dark forest; rather, they live on its perimeter in the partially open fields around the forest.

Therefore, providing some areas that are relatively open around the pond is also essential. When trying to attract animals, the goal is to decide what you want to attract and focus on those animals rather than try to attract everything.

Fox cubs and other young mammals may fall in garden ponds.

Unwanted Visitors

In this regard, there are many animals that you do not want to attract. Deer, rabbits, woodchucks, skunks, raccoons, and herons are all animals that typically should be dissuaded from taking up residence in your landscape. Deer can be highly destructive and eat just about any type of vegetation, especially in the winter when food becomes scarce. In the spring, they eay the young buds coming from trees or popping up from perennials, so they can dramatically reduce the growth of the young plants. They also tend to produce trails throughout the landscape, which can be very unsightly. Lastly they harbor the ticks that carry Lyme disease. For these reasons, attempts should be made to keep them from being regular visitors. This can include using scents from their predators.

Similarly woodchucks and rabbits can decimate a newly planted landscape. The two in combination can be especially damaging, as

Part 3

DO NOT play around with snakes. This is a venomous species called a Cottonmouth, *Agkistrodon piscivorus*.

they will eat many perennials down to the ground. They also propagate quickly, so unless their numbers are kept in check, they can be a real problem to a naturally planted landscape. Both of these animals build burrows that will be hidden throughout the landscape. Once the animal is trapped, the burrows should be searched for and destroyed. Otherwise new woodchucks or rabbits will rapidly take them up and the problem will start all over again.

Raccoons are problematic, as they can be predatory toward fish, while skunks are problematic due to their smell and the possibility of their carrying rabies. To reduce any problems from these animals, several things can be done. First, no food or other material should be allowed to decay near the landscape. Garbage can lids should be thoroughly tied down, and nothing edible should be left out where the skunks or raccoons can get it.

In order to prevent raccoons from catching prized fish, several steps should be taken. First, the pond should be relatively deep (over 2 feet at least). Second, the sides should not be sloping into this deep area, but they should be straight down. These two steps will make it more difficult for the raccoon to be able to catch the fish. There should also be hiding places on the bottom of the pond that will keep the raccoon from having easy access to the fish. Lastly there should not be any place for the raccoon to perch to catch the fish. The more difficult you make it for the raccoon to fish the less likely it will be for the raccoon to become a problem.

Raccoons can be problematic.

The last problematic visitors that you want to keep from becoming a problem are herons. These large, beautiful birds can decimate a pond of fish in a relatively short time. These birds are present across the US, and just about everyone with a pond can relay a story about how all their fish disappeared in a few nights. Unfortunately, because they fly from place to place, it is difficult to keep them away. Some things that can be done to keep them from becoming problematic include placing netting over the pond, making sure that the pond is at least 3 feet deep in some spots, providing hiding places for the fish, and keeping the slope of the sides as steep as possible to keep the heron from having a ready place from which to fish.

There has also been some reported success in using decoy herons on a pond to keep other herons away. Herons are very territorial, so if one heron is present, it will keep other herons away. These decoys will only work, however, if they are moved frequently. Otherwise, the other herons wise up and come to the pond anyway. It is also possible to keep herons away by attracting smaller, faster birds that do not tolerate herons in their territory. Jays, red-winged blackbirds, and crows are all intolerant of herons. The reason for this is that in addition to fish, other favorites of herons are baby birds. When a heron comes into a territory occupied by these birds, they will often nip and harass the heron the point that it will leave the area. This is just another reason why attracting these birds is beneficial to a pond.

Attracting wildlife to a pond does not take a lot of effort or planning. With a little thought to keeping things as natural as possible and through the use of native plants, it is possible to get a wide variety of animals to visit your pond on a regular basis. It is often more difficult for many of these animals to find water for drinking or bathing than it is for them to find food. Therefore, with a little extra planning, your pond can be a magnet from attracting a wide variety of animals and add to the total enjoyment of your pond.

Designer Ponds—
Making a Pond Unique

Part 3

If given the same equipment, landscape materials, and space, each person would still design a pond that would be unique and reflect their own personal styles and taste. This amount of uniqueness, however, varies depending on how the pond's designer or builder ties these ideas together.

This classic Japanese water garden has it all!

There are several components to setting up a pond that can be changed to make it different or to make it stand out. These include water, rockwork, lighting, fish, and plants. How these components are utilized determines the overall beauty of the pond and what sets it apart and makes it attractive. It is not necessary to use all of these things to make a pond attractive, as the design and construction of a pond can be relatively inexpensive and still have impact on the viewer. Cost is not the telling feature that determines whether a pond is appealing or not.

The attribute that seems to make a good pond great is the effort that the owner puts into it. Even when a lot of money is spent on design and construction, this does not make a pond special unless the owner puts effort into maintaining it and keeping everything in balance over a period of time. Even when an outside maintenance company performs its duty regularly, most ponds still seem to lose some of their sparkle over time. The reason for this is probably due to the fact that a pond is a work in progress and needs the efforts of its owner to really shine. It is never complete or finished unless someone observes it closely and regularly and interacts with it daily. Without the owner's attention, a pond will never attain the beauty of one that is closely supervised.

Creating Your Own Style

When designing and constructing a landscape that will incorporate water, the first thing to be considered is the pond and how it will fit into the overall landscape. In any landscape, the pond is more than just a small area that will hold water–it is often the focal point for the garden itself. A pond should never be a non-moving item, and in even a simple setup, at least some movement needs to occur, and this is what makes even a small pond stand out.

Dr. Hiroaki Otsuki from Fukui, Japan, designed this pond with the safety of children and large animals in mind.

By being a reservoir, it is the center of activity. This activity can be as simple as the movement of water out of a small fountain within the pond or moving water above the pond and having it splash back in (i.e. waterfalls or cascades). Or it can be the end point for a stream that moves water gradually down a shallow slope and back into the pond in constant fashion. Regardless of which type of movement is chosen, having motion within and around the pond produces multiple effects. Water motion is a natural attractant for both people and animals. When people see and hear water moving, it draws them to it. This is probably why waterfalls and fountains are becoming more and more popular.

Importance of Water Movement

Having constant water movement in a yard is not only a source of visual enjoyment, but it is also very relaxing. Water movement also produces beneficial effects for the pond as well. It helps to aerate the

Part 3

These koi are enjoying spacious quarters with excellent water flow.

pond, increasing its oxygen content and keeping the water from becoming stagnant. Stagnant water often attracts mosquitos and can develop unappealing odors, making your pond look and smell like a cesspool rather than the beautiful focal point of your garden. Water movement keeps the fish and other inhabitants of the pond healthy and can also keep the pond cooler by allowing for greater evaporation, which can be crucial during the hot, summer months.

Pond Kits

The first aspect to add to a pond's appeal that should be planned for is what type of water movement is going to occur. For small ponds or for those located where there is limited space, the obvious choice is to include a fountain in the pond. It is now relatively easy to include a fountain in a pond, and kits for this purpose are now widely available at most retail garden-supply stores or anywhere garden ponds are sold. These kits should include a small, submersible pump and tubing that allows the pump to disperse the water above the pond.

These kits can also include statuary that stand above the pond, small diameter pipes that spray the water in different patterns above the pond, or even elaborate metal pipes that produce ever-changing patterns of water spray. Regardless of which type of fountain is chosen, the goal is to keep the water in constant motion and also to keep the water within the pond itself. It is a common mistake for people who desire to make their own garden pond kit to choose a pump that spits water halfway across the yard–another good reason to

Pond kits, like this one, are particularly helpful for beginners.

buy a ready-made kit. These fountains produce no benefit if they do not keep the water within the pond, so before adding a fountain, make sure that it is sized to match the size of the pond and that it looks appropriate in that pond. If the pond is only 4 feet square, it makes no sense to have a fountain that sprays water over an area that is greater than 2 feet square.

The fountain has to be in proper perspective to the size of the pond in which it is located. A pond with an appropriately sized fountain can be placed just about anywhere. This allows this type of water based landscape device to be included into just about every landscape.

Optional Water Features

While a pond with a fountain can be enjoyable to view, one that

The source is a point before the stream where the water originates.

includes a stream and/or waterfall is even more pleasing to the eye. It should be noted, however, that unlike a pond with a fountain that can be constructed out of plastic and placed just about anywhere, Dry Streambeds and Heavy Rocks are usually more permanent in nature and, as a result, they become more a part of the landscape and have greater impact on the viewer.

Dry Streambeds

When planning for wet streams it may also be a good idea to have a dry streambed put in along the wet streambed. This will not only add an additional natural component to the landscape, but it will also provide for drainage for when the stream or pond overflow. All that is really necessary is to have a shallow narrow canal adjacent to the lower pond or higher areas where water pools that allow for runoff. This dry streambed should be planed with plants that like "wet feet" near its lower regions and with plants that like drier soil in the higher regions. It should be filled with rocks similar to those that are placed in the wet stream (river rock).

The key with these is to keep them in perspective. This stream should be smaller but in the same scale as the wet stream. Therefore, if the wet stream is small and narrow with small rocks, that is what should be used here. If, however, the wet stream is large, then the dry streambed should also be large and then it can contain boulders and other large rocks just like the wet stream. The goal of the dry streambed is both functional and aesthetic. It provides an additional point of interest to the wet stream, and it functions to move excess water away from the stream to a desired area.

In order to get the impact of flowing water, the stream does not have to be overly deep. As long as the bed is at least an inch or two deep along most of its path and a foot or so in the pooling areas, it should be fine. The stream can either be designed to allow for a continuous drop, or there can be areas where the water drops off more dramatically. For maximum impact, small or large waterfalls can also be incorporated into the design.

Rocks and Other Construction Materials

Even though the water portion of a landscape will be the dominant feature, there are still several other components that help to make a pond-based landscape stand out. Next among these is the rockwork incorporated into the pond. For most ponds, the rock type that is chosen should have both boulder shapes of varying sizes as well as flat stones, and all should be of similar colors. This is necessary so that the rocks that are incorporated into the pond and stream look similar to those that are used in the waterfalls and walkways.

If differently colored rocks are used, it is not appealing, and the overall effect is out of balance. To balance things even more, the rocks should be similar to those that are already incorporated into the overall landscape. These rocks should also be in scale to the size

Pond enthusiasts have a wide variety of decorative rocks from which to choose from.

of the water feature and the overall landscape. A large waterfall that is made up of tiny stones looks out of balance, as does a small stream filled with large boulders. Therefore, for water features to be pleasing, the rockwork has to be in scale.

Similarly, the construction materials used with the rock also need to be in balance and blended to look natural. If gray mortar is used to cement beige rocks, this diminishes from the water feature. Therefore, as with everything else, the look has to be natural, so if mortar is going to be used where it will be seen, then it will need to be dyed to match the colors of the rocks. In similar fashion any pumps, plumbing, or filters that will be used will need to be hidden from view. There are many means to do this, including hollow fiberglass, Styrofoam rocks, or logs, into which these items can be placed. Obviously, the more closely these items look to other items incorporated into the landscape, the more natural the pond will look.

Using Plants

In terms of providing a natural look, except for the pond itself, nothing adds to the naturalness of a pond more than a natural-looking planting. Choosing specific plants to complement a landscape and a water feature is an individual decision, but some rules are helpful. First, native plants should be the first choice. Native plants have the greatest likelihood for survival and they will attract more native animals than will non-natives. In addition, they have a far greater likelihood of surviving and growing in to make the pond look more natural over time. They are also more likely to blend in with the other plants growing around the pond.

A wide assortment of plants may be used to create various effects.

All plants should be planted in groups of three or five. Single plants look isolated and two plants produce conflict. Also, the number of different plants chosen should be limited. A large-massed planting of same-species plants usually looks better than small groups of different species of plants. Plants can also be massed according to their complements in terms of their coloration and bloom time. Plants can also be complementary in terms of their leaf structures and the coloration of their foliage. Tall plants should be placed toward the back or behind a pond or stream to provide a backdrop. Short plants should be toward the front or in front of the pond to soften the edges but not to impede the view of the pond. Plants

Part 3

should be placed so that some are in every environment within the pond, while some should be immersed within the pond itself and others on both sides of the pond as would occur in nature.

Virtually every nook around the pond should have something growing in it, as would be the case in nature; otherwise, it looks like the pond was just suddenly dropped into place. Plants should provide a sense of harmony within the pond. They cannot only be used to hide things, but with careful planning and planting, they can also be used to focus attention on the pond by acting to frame things.

Tropical Fish Hobbyist

The leading aquarium keeping magazine, Tropical Fish Hobbyist has been the source of accurate, up-to-the minute, fascinating information on every facet of the aquarium hobby including freshwater fish, aquatic plants, marine aquaria, mini-reefs, and ponds for over 50 years. TFH will take you to new heights with its informative articles and stunning photos. With thousands of fish, plants, and other underwater creatures available, the hobbyist needs levelheaded advice about their care, maintenance, and breeding. TFH authors have the knowledge and experience to help make your aquarium sensational.

P.O. Box 427

Neptune, NJ 07754-9989

For subscription information please e-mail:

info@tfh.com

or call:

1-888-859-9034

Piedmont Koi & Watergarden Society

Geoffrey Huntley - President

E-Mail: president@remove.pkwsonline.com

Water World

Water World is a company that specializes in koi ponds, fish, plants, as well as a full line of accessories. They also offer expert advice from professionals that have been in the business for many years. They are located at:

Water World at Monmouth Feed

294 Squankum Road

Farmingdale, NJ 07727

Or you can visit them on the web:

www.waterworldonline.com

Index

A

Aerobic bacteria, 98

Algae blooms, 18

American arrowhead, 82

Ammonia, 15, 98

Amphibians, 34, 132-133

Anacharis, 120

Aquatic morning glory, 124

Arrowhead, 124

Astilbe, 68

Azaleas, 68, 82

Azolla caroliniana, 120

B

Bacopa caroliniana, 124

Bacopa, 124

Bamboo, 92

Biological filtration, 15-17, 98

Birdbaths, 78

Birds, 34-35, 68, 97, 134-140

Black elephant ear, 121

Black magic taro, 124

Bleeding heart, 68

Bog filters, 123-126

Boxwood, 82, 108

Butterflies, 35, 68

Butterfly fern, 120

C

Canna spp., 83

Cardinal flower, 83

Cattails, 86, 121, 125

Chameleon plant, 124

Chipmunks, 35

Colocasia esculenta, 121

Cotoneaster, 68

Crocodiles, 64

Crocosmia spp., 83

Cyperus alternifolius, 84

Cyprinus carpio, 94

D

Dionae muscipula, 121

DLS, 15

Dragonflies, 33, 35, 68

Dry streambeds, 150-151

Duckweed, 120-121

E

Eichhornia crassipes, 83

Elodea spp., 120

English ivy, 69

Evergreens, 107-108

F

Fairy moss, 120

Ferns, 82

Floating hearts, 116

Floating ornaments, 64

Formal fountains, 58-59, 77

Formal pools, 57-58

Formal waterfalls, 59-60

Frog bit, 120

Frogs, 35, 64, 68

G

GFCIs, 22,

Golden club, 23

Goldfish, 24-25, 99

Gooseneck loosestrife, 126

Green water, 18

H

Hardy lilies, 111, 113

Hippos, 64

Holly, 82, 108

Horsetail rush, 124

Hosta, 68, 82, 126

Houttuynia cordata, 124

Hydrangeas, 82

I

Insects, 34, 130-132

Iris laevigata, 83

Iris versicolor, 124

J

Japanese maple, 69

K

Koi, 24-25, 56, 60, 87-89, 94-102, 148

L

Leaves, 13, 107-109, 112-113

Lemna minor, 120

Lepomis gibbosus, 35

Lysmachia nummilaria, 124

M

Mammals, 34, 68, 140-144

Mechanical filtration, 15-16, 98

Myrtle, 69

N

Nitrate, 98

Nitrite, 98

Nymphaea spp., 83, 85

Nymphaea xmarliacea, 83

Nymphoides peltata, 116

O

Oaks, 107

Orontium aquaticum, 23

Overwintering, 100-101

P

Pachysandra, 69

Picker rush, 121

Pines, 108

Pistia spp., 120

Pistia stratiotes, 119

Pontederia cordata, 121

Pontederia cordata, 124

Pumpkinseed, 35

Pumps, 17-18, 42-45, 76

Purple iris, 124

R

Raccoons, 97, 129, 141, 143

Recumbent yews, 68

Rhododendrons, 82

Rushes, 86

S

Sagittaria spp., 124

Salamanders, 64

Salvinia rotundifolia, 120

Sarracenia spp., 121

Sedges, 86

Sensitive plant, 124

Shubunkins, 24, 99

Skimmers, 18,

Snails, 64

Spouting ornaments, 64

Spreading junipers, 68

Submersible lights, 20

Surface lighting, 21

T

Tadpoles, 35

Trees, 13

Turtles, 35, 64

Typha angustifolia, 125

U

Ultraviolet sterilizers, 18

Umbrella palm, 124

Umbrella plant, 84

V

Venus flytrap, 121

Viburnum, 82

W

Water celery, 124

Water hyacinth, 56, 81-83, 118

Water irises, 82-83

Water lettuce, 118

Water lilies, 20, 23, 73, 80, 83, 85, 111-115

Water lotus, 115-116

Water zinnia, 124

Wheat germ, 101

Whiskey barrel, 70-71

Z

Zen garden, 91-92

Photo Credits

All Japan NISHIKI-GOI show, 27th Annual, 87-88, 95-96

Anita Nelson, 125

Derek Lambert, 54, 90

Dr. Bert Frank, 50

F. Rosenzweig, 99

G. Dibley, 143

G. Lurquin, 74

Dr. Herbert R. Axelrod, 49, 53, 81, 92

Hugh Nicholas, 79, 100

J. Tyson, 9, 106, 110, 126, 129

L. Wischnath, 132

M. Gilroy, 13, 23, 28, 32, 34, 70, 123, 141

M. Sweeney, 78

M.P. & C. Piednoir, 97, 122, 124

Maleta Walls, 116

Michael Smoker, 142

N. Fletcher, 17

Osamu Nobuhara, 105

Paul Bennett, 56

S. J. Smith, 24

Stapeley, 10, 12, 83, 85-86, 108-109,

T. Anne Barber, 21, 38-39, 42, 45, 59, 63, 149, 152

Ted Lannan, 27

TFH Archives, 15, 30, 35, 37, 46, 48, 58, 60-61, 65, 67-68, 72, 75, 112-113, 118-119, 121, 127, 133-134, 136, 139

Zen Nippon Airinkai, 89, 101, 145, 147-148, 153